FRUIT

FROM THE HEART

WISDOM FOR EVERY
SEASON OF LIFE

Written By:
John R. Thompson Sr.

ISBN-13: 978-0998802503
ISBN-10: 0998802506

Dudley Publishing House

www.dphouse.net

DEDICATIONS

With a deep sense of appreciation, I dedicate this book to the lover of my life, My Wife—Jenice—for your eternal and unfailing love and support. I am grateful that God has prepared us for each other. I love you more today than I did when we first met.

To my sons John R. and Justin R.: In the moment of your births until this very moment, you have been the joy of my life. I see in you the greatness that you shall become. My prayer for you is that God will mature you into the men that he has predestined for you to be, as He uses you for kingdom purpose. May you always look to him for his guidance, trust, and help as He reveals to you Himself. I love you.

To my granddaughter—Jeniel—you are the heartbeat of my day.

To my mother: My love for you is forever and always. God had a plan for us all the time. To My siblings: I love you dearly.

To my staff, CTCC family, and my supporters: Your amazing loyalty, commitment, and sacrifice are eternal.

ACKNOWLEDGMENTS

Father, you are my most precious and valued love. Thank you for my being alive in you. It is true if I had ten thousand tongues I could not thank you enough.

To Sam Augustine: You will never truly understand how you awakened, released and set me free. Thank you.

My wife and Co-Pastor—Jenice R. Thompson—you are my editor, grammar specialists, and teacher.

To my sons—John and Justin R. Thompson—thank you for the many debates over grammar, pronunciation, syntax, language, diction, and definitions. Your instructors taught you very well.

To Dudley Publishing House (DP HOUSE), Kenyon, and Jasmine Dudley, God has anointed you for the kingdom for such a time as this. My heart flutters with gratefulness for all that you do over at DP HOUSE. The many countless lives that will be changed because of what you do will be

realized for centuries to come and in eternity.

And I acknowledge everyone who didn't believe in me.

Thank you. You motivated me!

Contents

BOOK PRAISE

Navigating through life's journey can be so tedious. When we come into this world, we are not given a handbook to successful living to study. Instead, we are placed in life's classrooms to learn from its experiences. The believer, of course, has the word of God by which to govern one's pilgrimage, and in many cases we have our families and their beliefs, traditions, and upbringing from which we can draw enlightenment. In addition, if you are blessed to be united with a well-rounded, extrasensory, matured companion you are among the blessed. I said all that to introduce my companion and the author of this gem *Fruit From the Heart*, in the person of Bishop John R. Thompson, Sr.

I am so excited that he is finally beginning to share from his wealth of wisdom. This book is simple and practical. It lends itself as an easy read to readers and nonreaders alike. It's so refreshing because he drops jewels for everything from love, relationships, to your walk with God. As his wife of over thirty (30) years, I am humbled and extremely honored to say he is not just sharing wisdom via lip service; but this man lives by his own words every-single-day. His family—his sons John II, Justin, and I—can vouch for this. More recently he has been challenged—or should I say abundantly blessed—to take on the role as a Pop-Pop (grandfather) to our precious Jeniel, and it has only proven that his wealth of knowledge and compassion reaches further than our generation can see.

This timely treasure chest will prove to be a lifeline to you and yours in a plethora of ways. Its emphasis on relationships, character building, ministry and more is sure to challenge you to navigate through life's obstacles with greater ease. Sometimes all it takes is a new outlook on an old situation. While discouragements, disappointments and broken hearts are unavoidable, it is comforting to know he's someone who has been where you are, or he at least understands your plight. Bishop Thompson is able to offer precious golden nuggets that will help you continue to voyage on to your destiny. I love his famous mantra quoted in this book, "You'll never see a tree eat its own fruit." Because of this, he's willing to share his fruit with you. I hope you will do the same for others.

It is with great gladness that I highly recommend this book. I sense this book will be a wonderful addition to your self-help library.

Jenice R. Thompson

Co-Pastor, Calvary Temple Christian Center Ministries

First Lady of the International Royal Priesthood

Fellowship

FOREWORD

I have known John for over thirty years, and I have seen his ministry grow exponentially! We often erroneously think of the significance and growth of ministry by *mega*. However, it is very possible that we have *mega* and not minister. An example of this are those who simply regurgitate what we know and not what people need. John's ministry's significance and growth is his *mega* anointing to apply the Word and minister without gimmick.

Through the years John has expostulated the Word of God with the enthusiasm of a preacher whose mission is to bring spiritual and psychological health to the community he serves.

With this book John's community now expands his exegetical ministry to the world, in a form that can be revisited in meditation day-to-day.

Now John has taken us—through this book to— theology and psychology in dichotomy. This book instructs through the scriptures the essential need for tranquility in our thoughts about ourselves, as it relates to decision-making. What is more fundamental to a Christian's existence than the decisions he or her makes? He seriously gives insight into how whether certain of my choices can displease God, but my life as whole does not! He brings us into the peace of God when he insists the child of God understand that we should not look at ourselves in pieces but as a whole: "All things work together as a whole..."

Thank God for this book that instructs me to seek the way of God but not to be self-condemnatory as I travel from decision to decision. The thought of agonizing in one's decision-making—for fear of one's life spiraling out of control—is quickly dispensed within this work. This book is a must read for anyone who has been psychologically debilitated because of their choices. You will be on the road to recovery.

Fruit from the Heart will help you to get to a place of personal tranquility in the middle of a tumultuous world. Thanks for blessing us with your *mega* anointing John!

Bishop Noel Jones

Senior Pastor, City of Refuge Church (Gardena, CA)

Noel Jones Ministries

Introduction
"Fruit from the Heart"

The lack of a roadmap in life has left many people distressed and lost. I have found that there are many who worry about the decisions they've made in life. Feelings of insecurity about their choices and the dissatisfaction of bad judgment calls haunt most people daily. Have you ever felt as if your life isn't pleasing to God? Do you ever feel as though the choices you've made in life aren't acceptable to God? Do you know how many people are just like you? There are many—that I can't even number—who secretly believe that they do not deserve success or happiness because of their decisions in life. Harboring fears that you are not wise enough, knowledgeable enough, or just plain good enough. Sound familiar?

This groundbreaking book reveals the heart of a general in the Kingdom, and the wisdom I have gathered from forty-three years of walking in the faith. Throughout this book, I will offer you knowledge in the form of diamonds, nuggets—or as I like to call them—precious fruit. It is certainly my hope and prayer that these principles shared will assist you in resolving your personal dilemmas. I want to build your confidence and faith; by sharing with you precious truths that I've learned along the way. For every believer in Christ who has yearned to grow, mature, to be strengthened and built in their faith, "Fruit from the Heart" is a truly invaluable and effective well of living water for you.

This book combines wisdom, faith, and strength with a no-nonsense approach that is sure to foster individual growth. It's "Fruit from My Heart."

"They shall still bring forth fruit in old age; they shall be

fat and flourishing."

Psalm 92:14 (KJV)

"And he shall be like a tree planted by the rivers of water, which bringeth forth his fruit in his season; his leaf also shall not wither, and whatsoever he doeth shall prosper."

Psalm 1:3 (KJV)

1

Character

Fruit #1: "I will make your name great; but until that happens develop your character."

Reflections for the Day:

_____

_____

_____

_____

_____

_____

_____

_____

Fruit #2: "What's greater: character or anointing?"

Reflections for the Day:

_____

_____

_____

_____

_____

_____

_____

_____

_____

_____

_____

_____

_____

Fruit #3: "The hardest people to reach with the love of God is not the "bad people." They know that they have issues. They have no defense. The hardest ones to win for God are the self-righteous and arrogant people. They just can't see themselves. They can't bring themselves to believe they have such a flaw within themselves."

Reflections for the Day:

_____

_____

_____

_____

_____

_____

_____

_____

Fruit #4: "PLEASE TAKE NOTE: You may have the greatest gift around town that blesses everyone who comes in contact with it, but if your attitude is nasty then you really have nothing. Your business may be the best in town, but if you're rude then you really have nothing at all. Your ministry could be immaculate. You may be unmatched in everything you do, but if you are proud and haughty then you have absolutely nothing. I have news for you. You can be replaced. There's somebody out there better at what you do. People will find someone else. Yes, it's nice to be gifted, but it's more important to have character."

Reflections for the Day:

_____

_____

_____

_____

Fruit #5: "Your gift will get you in the door, but it's only

your character that will sustain you on your next level."

Reflections for the Day:

_____

_____

_____

_____

_____

_____

_____

_____

_____

_____

_____

_____

_____

2

Faith

Fruit 6: "As long as you are fighting; it hasn't conquered you!"

Reflections for the Day:

_____

_____

_____

_____

_____

_____

_____

Fruit #7: "The promise is already assigned to you. Your name is on it. It's just waiting on you to have faith enough to come and take it by force."

Reflections for the Day:

_____

_____

_____

_____

_____

_____

_____

_____

_____

_____

Fruit #8: "You might be behind, but there's always a

comeback."

Reflections for the Day:

_____

_____

_____

_____

_____

_____

_____

_____

_____

_____

_____

_____

Fruit #9: "I'm at my best when I believe."

Reflections for the Day:

_____

_____

_____

_____

_____

_____

_____

_____

_____

_____

_____

_____

_____

_____

_____

Fruit #10: "Just because there's nothing happening it doesn't mean there's nothing happening. Remember, when you're drilling for oil there is a period of anticipation just before the breakthrough."

Reflections for the Day:

_____

_____

_____

_____

_____

_____

_____

_____

_____

_____

Fruit #11: "We are victory. We walk like victory. We talk like victory. We sound like victory."

Reflections for the Day:

_____

_____

_____

_____

_____

_____

_____

_____

_____

_____

_____

_____

Fruit #12: "No matter how weak you are in faith right now.

Trust that God will send someone with a word to lift you.

That's the nature of God. That's how He operates. He'll

never leave you without a word that will lift you and

liberate you. Have faith."

Reflections for the Day:

_____

_____

_____

_____

_____

_____

_____

_____

_____

Fruit #13: "A believer in the home, work place, and community is one of the greatest powers on earth. Satan hates you, but God delights in you. God is excited about you. So take your place. Stand for righteousness and be the salt. Use your power to make a difference."

Reflections for the Day:

_____

_____

_____

_____

_____

_____

_____

_____

_____

Fruit #14: "The only thing that stands between you and what God has for you—now that your faith is alive and well—is diligence. Fight the spirit of laziness and apathy."

Reflection for the Day:

_____

_____

_____

_____

_____

_____

_____

_____

_____

_____

Fruit #15: "Faith is not about success or failure. It's about

trust."

Reflections for the Day:

Fruit #16: "Even in our mistakes we are prosperous because they show us the magnitude of how much faith we have. Our faith shows us the investments we've made toward our survival."

Reflection for the Day:

_____

_____

_____

_____

_____

_____

_____

_____

_____

_____

Fruit #17: "Winners redefine records, set new standards,

force us into the future, and set bars for the unborn

generations to come. Be a winner!"

Reflections for the Day:

_____

_____

_____

_____

_____

_____

_____

_____

_____

_____

Fruit #18: "A man of faith is a dangerous man. He has something backing him. That something is the power of God."

Reflections for the Day:

_____

_____

_____

_____

_____

_____

_____

_____

_____

_____

Fruit #19: "Have you ever ordered something and received a confirmation number or receipt for it? Well, just open your Bible. Herein lies over three-thousand promises that you could claim as yours today. Your faith is your confirmation number and receipt that it's already ordered for you. "Let's not get weary in well doing; for in due season [at the right time of manifestation], ye shall reap (Galatians 6:9)." You just can't faint in your faith—or the way I like to put it—lose your faith."

Reflections for the Day:

_____

_____

_____

_____

_____

_____

Fruit #20: "If it all falls apart when you start to pick up a matter; know that all things are under God's watchful eyes. And He never blinks. God is watching over you and His word to perform just what He said. I promise."

Reflections for the Day:

_____

_____

_____

_____

_____

_____

_____

_____

_____

_____

Fruit #21: "Your disappointment is nothing but proof that you had faith. If you didn't expect something greater then you wouldn't have been disappointed. The very fact that you disagreed with the outcome means your faith is at work. Know this, it wasn't your faith that was disappointed; it was your mind. Your faith was only tried and strengthened. Disappointments strengthen your faith."

Reflections for the Day:

_____

_____

_____

_____

_____

_____

_____

Fruit #22: "I had a dream once. It was a dream that I was holding a bundle of money. In the dream I spoke to myself and said, "When you wake up from your sleep, you will still have this money in your hand. Now wake up." When I woke up, I had no physical money in my hand at the time. This is how faith works. You have to go into the spiritual realm, see it, and believe it whole-heartedly there first. Connect with the spirit of God that will tell you the promise is yours. Once you've connected, then by faith pull it out of the spirit into the natural."

Reflections for the Day:

_____

_____

_____

_____

_____

Fruit #23: "There are no limits to what God can do for mankind; except the limits we place on Him. Take the limits off of God. Take Him out of the box; and He'll do something super abundant. God has a supply of more than enough."

Reflections for the Day:

_____

_____

_____

_____

_____

_____

_____

_____

_____

_____

Fruit #24: "Command—in faith—the promises of God. Trust and wait on God to perform them. By your obedience to His word stay away from the practice of sin. And diligently work to see the fulfillment of His promise; even if you have to fight to possess it."

Reflections for the Day:

_____

_____

_____

_____

_____

_____

_____

_____

_____

_____

Fruit #25: "Faith is likened unto this: a child creates scribble dibble abstract chaos on a piece of paper and calls it art; only for the parent to build their esteem and confidence by praising them and placing the art on the refrigerator. So it is with the Father and your faith. To many, your faith looks like scribble dibble abstract chaos; but God sees a masterpiece (childlike faith) and He honors that."

Reflections for the Day:

_____

_____

_____

_____

_____

_____

_____

_____

Fruit #26: "Trust God in all things."

Reflections for the Day:

_____

_____

_____

_____

_____

_____

_____

_____

_____

_____

_____

_____

_____

Fruit #27: "There was one last faith bone in your body that had to be strengthened before you could carry the weight of this next blessing. The weight of this next blessing is so heavy that you can't even imagine carrying it in your current state. This is why God had to allow horrible situations to occur in your life. This wasn't to kill you. This was to strengthen your faith bones and muscles to carry the weight of this next glory."

Reflections for the Day:

_____

_____

_____

_____

_____

_____

_____

3
Family

Fruit #28: "Outside of your relationship with God there is nothing more important than investing quality time in your family."

Reflections for the Day:

_____

_____

_____

_____

_____

_____

_____

_____

Fruit #29: "Holidays—like Thanksgiving—are a perfect opportunity to gather family at the table at a set time. Before you allow anyone to touch a plate require each family member to say, "I love you." Don't let the enemy steal these divine moments from you."

Reflections for the Day:

_____

_____

_____

_____

_____

_____

_____

_____

_____

Fruit #30: "When people who are supposed to be your family talk about you like a dog and they say things that have nothing to do with your behavior or character just worship the Lord. Then smile at them. This is what confuses ignorant people and the enemy too."

Reflections for the Day:

_____

_____

_____

_____

_____

_____

_____

_____

_____

_____

Fruit #31: "Family will do things to lift you; but most family will do things that get you down. Recognize that their only human. They're not going to always do everything perfect. Release the fear of them hurting you. Release the shame. Forgive them of all discrepancies and violations. Release them of their faults. Choose to love them with the love of Christ. Enjoy every God-given moment with them. Each day you see them is a God-given moment. Seize the day. You might not ever get these moments back again."

Reflections for the Day:

_____

_____

_____

_____

_____

_____

Fruit #32: "Which is first? Family or ministry? Many will scream, "Of course family comes first Bishop!" Question: then why does your spouse feel like a mistress? Tell me, why do your children hate the church so much? One preacher I know actually sent his children away because— according to him—they had devils and were trying to block his purpose. "They needed too much attention," he says. Isn't it funny how we are anointed to save the whole world; but can't even save our own families? Family is your first ministry."

Reflections for the Day:

_____

_____

_____

_____

_____

Fruit #33: "I'm a bit confused. We hold grudges and bitterness in our heart against our family members and those closest to us. We allow Satan to fill our hearts with separation; but then when we get a phone call about one of their deaths we cry and act a plum fool. Let not your hearts deceive you brethren. Right now—today—we have a chance to love them and hold them. "Let not the sun go down on your wrath (Ephesians 4:26)."

Reflections for the Day:

_____

_____

_____

_____

_____

_____

_____

4

Fear

Fruit #34: "You can be gifted, anointed, called, and still

controlled by fear. Fear limits what God can perform in

your life. Fear is a sign of disbelief. That's why you're so

powerful; but haven't produced anything yet. Divorce

fear!"

Reflections for the Day:

_____

_____

_____

_____

_____

_____

_____

Fruit #35: "Stop allowing other people's fear to control the steps you take. As long as you're in the will of God; do what's best for you. And above all, know that God is happy with your faith steps."

Reflections for the Day:

_____

_____

_____

_____

_____

_____

_____

_____

_____

_____

Fruit #36: "Fear dictates and captivates your anointing.

Defeat the fear; release the anointing!"

Reflections for the Day:

_____

_____

_____

_____

_____

_____

_____

_____

_____

_____

_____

_____

5

Forgiveness

Fruit #37: "Whenever God asks you to do something that you feel you can't; it's because He wants you to depend on Him to do it. I had to forgive the man that murdered my brother. I can remember standing about five feet away from him in the store. I could've easily retaliated. But it took the help and power of God to bring me to forgiveness. Hating and harboring is easy. It's the forgiving that takes divine power."

Reflections for the Day:

_____

_____

_____

_____

Fruit #38: "How can we forgive all sorts of leaders, kings, prophets, and such who committed ridiculous sins in the Bible, but fail to forgive our current pastors and leaders for their shortcomings? Sounds like a contradiction to me."

Reflections for the Day:

_____

_____

_____

_____

_____

_____

_____

_____

_____

Fruit #39: "When people hurt us, we want them to pay for it. Well, someone already has. Over two thousand years on Calvary's cross Jesus the Christ paid the wages of sin for all humanity. So be careful not to operate in witchcraft. To go beyond what Jesus did on the cross and make others pay for what they did to you is rebellion and an act of pride. You are in essence saying that what Christ did on Calvary wasn't enough to vindicate you and cover the flaws of the person who violated you. Not telling you to forget. Just telling you to forgive."

Reflections for the Day:

_____

_____

_____

_____

_____

Fruit #40: "Allow me to elaborate on forgiveness. In some special cases forgiveness is not so simple to extend. In cases like this spiritual advisement and counseling therapy may need to be your mode of action."

Reflections for the Day:

_____

_____

_____

_____

_____

_____

_____

_____

_____

_____

6

Growth

Fruit #41: "One of life's greatest tragedies is immature people who play with adult responsibilities like toys. They shoot guns like they're playing video games; never stopping to consider the very real consequences and ramifications of taking a life. They have babies; yet drop them and leave them like a child does a play doll when they're done playing with it. These type of people never stop to think about the emotional wounds these children will develop as a result of their neglect. Immature people run around town playing hide-and-go-seek with sexually transmitted infections. They have casual sex and conduct other degrading acts not really stopping to think about the consequences their actions could potentially garner like "going to bed early." By that I mean premature death. There are adults who have the mind of a child. They neglect their own children for instant gratification. They

have sleepovers with emotional promises; using their

bodies to make promises that their mouths never speak.

They want everything they see; yet not willing to go get a

job and pay for it to become a reality. One of life's

greatest tragedies is immature people who play with adult

responsibilities. If this is you; then game over. Why don't

you call it quits and decide to grow up today."

Reflections for the Day:

_____

_____

_____

_____

_____

_____

_____

Fruit #42: "People love the fruit of hard word; but not the process of planting, cultivating, and harvesting. These processes take time. Time takes maturity."

Reflections for the Day:

_____

_____

_____

_____

_____

_____

_____

_____

_____

_____

_____

7

Love

Fruit #43: "Knowing the love of God is the greatest love of all. The love of self is the second greatest love of all. Love of family is the third greatest love of all. But if you never learn to love yourself and if you never master the love of family; God's love can make up for it all."

Reflections for the Day:

_____

_____

_____

_____

_____

_____

_____

Fruit #44: "Don't miss the opportunity to tell a loved one

that you love them; by letting them die and never saying

so."

Reflections for the Day:

_____

_____

_____

_____

_____

_____

_____

_____

_____

_____

Fruit #45: "When the Bible says that, "God is love," it's referencing agape. God's love is beyond the limitations of erotica or brotherly love. It's agape."

Reflections for the Day:

_____

_____

_____

_____

_____

_____

_____

_____

_____

_____

_____

8

Marriage

Fruit #46: "Everyone considers the Jones's marriage to be a match made-in-heaven; when in actuality the couple has a front row seat next to the fireplace in hell. The moral of the story is: don't envy what looks perfect from across the street while wearing out-of-date bifocals! You really don't know what goes on behind closed doors. Just be sure to tend to your own home. Be sure that there is peace in your own home. That should be your main priority in a marriage."

Reflections for the Day:

_____

_____

Fruit #47: "In some marriages you have to push it in order for it to go. In others you have to carry it until it's able to walk on its own. Some marriages require you to sit in the ICU waiting room praying and crying—holding on to your last ounce of faith—until it resurrects again. Marriage requires different levels of faith. Which level is yours calling for?"

Reflections for the Day:

_____

_____

_____

_____

_____

_____

_____

Fruit #48: "I've learned this wisdom in life: if you start loving the man or woman more than you hate the issue they struggle with, that issue will become that much smaller and obsolete."

Reflections for the Day:

_____

_____

_____

_____

_____

_____

_____

_____

_____

_____

Fruit #49: To My Wife,

"You are the most beautiful person I know. Your essence and dimensions are stacked level high. Your foundation is as sweet as honey. Filled with true compassion and honesty is your heart. Your devotion is as authentic and genuine as real diamonds. I've loved you for many years— as teens and now as adults—and I still do. Happy twenty-third anniversary. Baby, I still love you."

To the Reader,

"Never forget to remind them why you married them. It's a sure way to keep you together and keep you loving."

Reflection of the Day:

_____

_____

_____

_____

Fruit #50: To My Wife,

"God must have thought I was someone special; because He gave me you. Although we began without much money; we had a whole lot of love. We've been broken and without many times. Like the time we lost so much when we had to bury our daughter. But then God gave us two beautiful sons. We've cried together until we laughed; and laughed together until we cried. We've shared twenty-four years of loving one another and growing through adversity. I wouldn't trade you for anything in the world. I love you now and forever baby."

To the Reader,

"Marriage has its hills and valleys. Marriage also consists of mountains and canyons. There will be up times and you can count on the low times too. But one thing is for sure, if you learn to love and mature you can ride any wave [whether you're on top or feeling low]."

Reflections for the Day:

_____

_____

_____

_____

_____

_____

_____

_____

_____

_____

_____

_____

_____

Fruit #51: "Once, I witnessed some young guys fixing their motor bike. One had done all of the work on the engine. Then he spent about an half hour priming the motor. But out of frustration he walked away. The engine just wouldn't start. Another kid came over and kicked the motor bike twice, and it started right up. Everyone gave him all the praise for getting the motor bike to start. How many of you have been in relationships with a person and then divorced them out of frustration; only to find out that someone else came by to jumpstart the person into their deliverance and greatness? Now the new person's getting all of the praise. Don't leave. You've done all of the hard work. All they need is a little kick and jumpstart."

Reflections for the Day:

_____

_____

_____

Fruit #52: To My Wife,

"I've loved you more than twenty-four years. It seems like we just began. I remember the day we got married. It rained so hard. I can recall watching you walk down the aisle. I thought to myself, "She's so beautiful. If only I could make her life wonderful." Sweetheart, I can only hope that I've done that for you so far. I can remember about a week before our wedding we decided to call everything off. But I knew that I couldn't live without you."

To the Reader,

"So you think you want to call it quits? Think again. If it's true love it'll stand the tests of time; because the love will never fail."

Reflections for the Day:

_____

_____

_____

_____

_____

_____

_____

_____

_____

_____

_____

_____

_____

_____

_____

_____

_____

_____

_____

_____

9

Pain

Fruit #53: "There is a pain that I can't explain. I shall never attempt to describe it. It's the pain of the loss of someone you love. The only thing I can say about this is that only God can help you mature as you endure."

Reflections for the Day:

_____

_____

_____

_____

_____

_____

Fruit #54: "There are benefits in burdens."

Reflections for the Day:

_____

_____

_____

_____

_____

_____

_____

_____

_____

_____

_____

_____

_____

Fruit #55: "God will remove your pain in such a complete

way that you won't even be able to remember how bad it

felt in the first place."

Reflections for the Day:

_____

_____

_____

_____

_____

_____

_____

_____

_____

_____

_____

Fruit #56: "The pain found you, but don't let it define

you."

Reflections for the Day:

_____

_____

_____

_____

_____

_____

_____

_____

_____

_____

_____

_____

_____

10

Parenthood

Fruit #57: "I can still remember when my wife and I drove our son up to University of Connecticut. When we finally got him to the campus we were able to get him all settled in. I can still remember having to fight back the tears as I watched my wife cry a river. She didn't want to leave him, and honestly neither did I. I stood there remembering the day that I stood next to my wife as she gave birth to this boy. Now there I was standing next to her on the campus of UCONN watching her give birth to a man. At that very moment I realized what it was to actually be a father."

Reflections for the Day:

_____

_____

_____

_____

_____

_____

_____

_____

_____

_____

_____

_____

_____

_____

Fruit #58: "You've got to have pain to release power."

Reflections for the Day:

_____

_____

_____

_____

_____

_____

_____

_____

_____

_____

_____

_____

Fruit #59: "The enemy wants to stress you out when it

comes to your kids. He wants to press you down to the

point that you speak against your children and their

destinies. DON'T DO IT! If so, you'll give the enemy the

right to carry out the assignment (the curse) that you speak

over them. "

Reflections for the Day:

_____

_____

_____

_____

_____

_____

_____

_____

Fruit #60: "My wife and I lost our daughter at childbirth

on December 10, 1990. She died just a few minutes before

birth. I miss her so, but I am grateful for the nine months we had her. Sometimes God will only allow you to have

nine months with them. Other times He'll allow you to

have a lifetime. No matter the length of time, cherish them,

learn from them, give them all you've got. But most of all,

let them change your life."

Reflections for the Day:

_____

_____

_____

_____

_____

_____

_____

11

Practical Wisdom

Fruit #61: "One season of preparation can change you forever."

Reflections for the Day:

_____

_____

_____

_____

_____

_____

_____

_____

Fruit #62: "You can't get anywhere in life allowing people to treat you the way they want to treat you. You have to teach people how to treat you. You must speak up and command respect. This is a message from Bishop John R. Thompson and I approve this message."

Reflections for the Day:

_____

_____

_____

_____

_____

_____

_____

_____

_____

Fruit #63: "Beware of the praise of men. It's the poison

used to gain the privilege of a relationship with you."

Reflections for the Day:

_____

_____

_____

_____

_____

_____

_____

_____

_____

_____

_____

_____

Fruit #64: "The more you focus, the more you produce.

The more you produce, the more you're promoted."

Reflections for the Day:

_____

_____

_____

_____

_____

_____

_____

_____

_____

_____

_____

_____

Fruit #65: "Just because you hold an office or position

doesn't mean you're living up to the standard in private."

Reflections for the Day:

_____

_____

_____

_____

_____

_____

_____

_____

_____

_____

_____

_____

_____

Fruit #66: "There's beauty in your brokenness. Look with

a different lens."

Reflections for the Day:

Fruit #67: "When I was a boy I used to think smoking was so cool. At the time, everybody in my family—even some friends—smoked. I thought to myself that it must've tasted good. The way they even held it was so cool to me. One day, one of my friends began to smoke and I asked him for a cigarette. I went over to the basketball court—where no one could see me—and I lit it up and took a puff. Oh my goodness! It burned my throat. I immediately became dizzy and nauseous. I was so sick that I had to go home and lie down. Needless to say, that was the end of my smoking days. The moral of the story is: everything that looks cool really isn't. And everything that everyone does really isn't for you."

Reflections for the Day:

_____

_____

_____

Fruit #68: "My praise is not predicated upon what I look

like in public, but rather what I survived in private."

Reflections for the Day:

Fruit #69: "You can't help the poor unless you are first rich. Think about this on all levels, not just financial."

Reflections for the Day:

_____

_____

_____

_____

_____

_____

_____

_____

_____

_____

_____

_____

Fruit #70: "Find the purpose behind you performing an

action and you'll find the strength to do it."

Reflections for the Day:

_____

_____

_____

_____

_____

_____

_____

_____

_____

_____

_____

_____

Fruit #71: "Never be afraid of hard work. It trains you to be a man or woman of faith. To work means you expect a favorable outcome every time."

Reflections for the Day:

_____

_____

_____

_____

_____

_____

_____

_____

_____

_____

_____

_____

Fruit #72: "Be careful not to always look at God as a

deliverer and miss that He's a sustainer."

Reflections for the Day:

_____

_____

_____

_____

_____

_____

_____

_____

_____

_____

Fruit #73: "A girl grows into a woman when she sees the needs of her family and begins to shop for those needs rather than just shop for her wants."

Reflections for the Day:

_____

_____

_____

_____

_____

_____

_____

_____

_____

_____

_____

_____

_____

Fruit #74: "Here it is in a nutshell: the attributes of the

Holy Ghost are righteousness, joy, and peace. The

attributes of the opposite are sin, depression, and drama."

Reflections for the Day:

_____

_____

_____

_____

_____

_____

_____

_____

_____

_____

_____

_____

Fruit #75: "You can't swim unless you jump in the water."

Reflections for the Day:

_____

_____

_____

_____

_____

_____

_____

_____

_____

_____

_____

_____

_____

_____

_____

_____

Fruit #76: "I never took a straight path anywhere. There will be bumps, potholes, curves, turns, traffic, stoplights, and re-routes for sure."

Reflections for the Day:

_____

_____

_____

_____

_____

_____

_____

_____

_____

_____

_____

_____

_____

Fruit #77: "It's not called running. It's called preparing.

Don't slow down unless it's God."

Reflections for the Day:

_____

_____

_____

_____

_____

_____

_____

_____

_____

_____

_____

_____

_____

_____

Fruit #78: "Choose to love even in the moments when you

struggle."

Reflections for the Day:

_____

_____

_____

_____

_____

_____

_____

_____

_____

_____

_____

_____

_____

Fruit #79: "There's a reason why the rearview mirror is

smaller than the windshield."

Reflections for the Day:

_____

_____

_____

_____

_____

_____

_____

_____

_____

_____

_____

_____

_____

_____

Fruit #80: "Everything may not be what you want it to be,

but thank God that it's not what it used to be."

Reflections for the Day:

_____

_____

_____

_____

_____

_____

_____

_____

_____

_____

_____

_____

Fruit #81: "The purpose of battle is to occupy."

Reflections for the Day:

_____

_____

_____

_____

_____

_____

_____

_____

_____

_____

_____

_____

_____

Fruit #82: "Be wise enough to depend on God."

Reflections for the Day:

_____

_____

_____

_____

_____

_____

_____

_____

_____

_____

_____

_____

_____

Fruit #83: "It's not about perfection. It's about perfectly

loving the imperfect."

Reflections for the Day:

_____

_____

_____

_____

_____

_____

_____

_____

_____

_____

_____

_____

_____

Fruit #84: "You can hear a story for so long that you'll begin to unconsciously adopt that story as your own. Be careful which stories you rehearse."

Reflections for the Day:

_____

_____

_____

_____

_____

_____

_____

_____

_____

_____

_____

_____

Fruit #85: "Truth be told, people don't like it when you tell the truth. Truth be told, those aren't the people for you. Truth must always be told, no matter how hard it might be to face."

Reflections for the Day:

_____

_____

_____

_____

_____

_____

_____

_____

_____

_____

_____

_____

Fruit #86: "The place you don't want to go—the places you

don't want to visit—are the places where your healing

resides."

Reflections for the Day:

_____

_____

_____

_____

_____

_____

_____

_____

_____

_____

_____

_____

Fruit #87: "People take notice when you do it with

excellence."

Reflections for the Day:

_____

_____

_____

_____

_____

_____

_____

_____

_____

_____

_____

_____

Fruit #88: "I'm convinced that we—as the Body of Christ—need to stop jumping, hollering, and shouting for a minute so that we could deal with the real underlying issues people face in the pews."

Reflections for the Day:

_____

_____

_____

_____

_____

_____

_____

_____

_____

_____

Fruit #89: "Respect the drama in people's lives. Stay away

and give it privacy."

Reflections for the Day:

_____

_____

_____

_____

_____

_____

_____

_____

_____

_____

_____

_____

_____

Fruit #90: "Stop trying to get everybody to help you make up your mind. Be courageous and make up your own mind."

Reflections for the Day:

_____

_____

_____

_____

_____

_____

_____

_____

_____

_____

_____

_____

Fruit #91: "Tears are memories running down your cheek,

that affect the heart."

Reflections for the Day:

_____

_____

_____

_____

_____

_____

_____

_____

_____

_____

_____

_____

_____

Fruit #92: "You have untapped power that you haven't used yet because the opportunity that will pull it out of you hasn't presented itself yet. Just wait and see."

Reflections for the Day:

_____

_____

_____

_____

_____

_____

_____

_____

_____

_____

Fruit #93: "You must fight past the negative perception that you have of yourself. What you think will ultimately be what you manifest. Your thoughts are ultimately, what is supposed to push you into your divine destiny and purpose. You are what God says you are. You are who God says you are. So see yourself God's way."

Reflections for the Day:

_____

_____

_____

_____

_____

_____

_____

_____

Fruit #94: "You know that you're mature in Christ when you begin to resist those things that you really want badly, but know that they aren't good for you. It's the season for strong minds. Start making destiny decisions and not deadly decisions."

Reflections for the Day:

_____

_____

_____

_____

_____

_____

_____

_____

_____

Fruit #95: "What God has given you grace to survive just might have killed someone else. Be thankful!"

Reflections for the Day:

_____

_____

_____

_____

_____

_____

_____

_____

_____

_____

_____

_____

Fruit #96: "Breaking others won't fix you."

Reflections for the Day:

_____

_____

_____

_____

_____

_____

_____

_____

_____

_____

_____

_____

Fruit #97: "Sometimes you just don't know what you want.

It's ok. Don't panic. That's why God's word and

revelation is there. Let them both be your guide."

Reflections for the Day:

_____

_____

_____

_____

_____

_____

_____

_____

_____

_____

_____

Fruit #98: "Whatever you are anointed to do, DO IT!"

Reflections for the Day:

_____

_____

_____

_____

_____

_____

_____

_____

_____

_____

_____

_____

_____

_____

Fruit #99: "Everything serves a purpose, if you let it."

Reflections for the Day:

_____

_____

_____

_____

_____

_____

_____

_____

_____

_____

_____

_____

_____

Fruit #100: "Choose the hard no or the easy yes. The hard no costs you temporary pain and discomfort but a lifetime of protection. The easy yes costs you temporary pleasure, but a lifetime of pain and regret."

Reflections for the Day:

_____

_____

_____

_____

_____

_____

_____

_____

_____

_____

Fruit #101: "Some people will never go to church.

Sometimes God will use you (the Church Body) to go to

them. That's my testimony. I'm so glad the church came to

where I was."

Reflections for the Day:

_____

_____

_____

_____

_____

_____

_____

_____

_____

_____

Fruit #102: "Everything is linked to behavior. Watch the behavior of a thing. This determines the nature of a thing."

Reflections for the Day:

_____

_____

_____

_____

_____

_____

_____

_____

_____

_____

_____

_____

Fruit #103: "Would you leave your church if your Pastor committed adultery, committed a conspiracy to commit murder, or even actually committed the act of murder itself? Nine times out of ten, you would. That's not how a man of God is supposed to act. Right? Would you leave your church if you caught your Pastor at the local party with wine being passed all around the building? What if you found out that your Pastor was best friends with some of the worldliest unclean politicians, tax collectors, and other seculars? You'd probably grow uneasy with your trusting his leadership. Right? Well, King David did most of these things and you still read the book of Psalms extrapolating life lessons from his writings. As a matter of fact, Jesus was the one who hung out at the parties and was friends with some of the greatest crooks in the city, but you still choose to serve Him. Let's be clear. This is not a license to sin. This is a license to be realistic. Yes, we are called to be holy and separate from the world. But that means separate in the things we do. We are not to totally remove ourselves from the midst of these type of people. Let's remember that we are the salt and we're supposed to be in the earth making it salty again."

Reflections for the Day:

_____

_____

_____

_____

_____

_____

_____

_____

_____

_____

Fruit #104: "When will you stop trying to be who you think God wants you to be, and start getting in His presence and allowing Him to love you for who He created you to be?"

Reflections for the Day:

_____

_____

_____

_____

_____

_____

_____

_____

_____

_____

_____

_____

Fruit #105: "One day I walked into the store to grab a couple of items. Once I got to the register, my total had come up to $11.06. So I gave the young man (the clerk) a $20 bill. I then realized that I wanted to give him six cents to make things even. So I reached in my pocket, but only found a dime. Once I handed it to the young man he looked confused and had a perplexed face. After I stood there for a while waiting on my change I finally realized that he didn't know how to give me my correct change. I subtly stated to the young man, "Son, give me $9.04 back in change." This broke my heart. The moral of this story is: young people please stay in school and get all you can. Be sure to get understanding as well. Your education is important to your wellbeing. You don't want to be taken advantage of just because you don't know something."

Reflections for the Day:

Fruit #106: "For years I struggled with who I was. I just didn't want to disappoint other people and who they thought I should be. I quickly learned that no one else's opinion should matter. If it does, you give control of your life over to them and they can shape and mold you as they please. Think about that."

Reflections for the Day:

_____

_____

_____

_____

_____

_____

_____

_____

Fruit #107: "Stop crossing oceans for people who won't

jump a puddle for you. Stop climbing mountains to help

those who won't even climb an anthill for you."

Reflections for the Day:

_____

_____

_____

_____

_____

_____

_____

_____

_____

_____

_____

Fruit #108: "Years ago a New York cartoonist drew a comic that had a dog typing away on a computer. The dog looked over at his master and says, "No one knows you're a dog on the Internet." Here's the moral of the story: You never who's hiding behind those words and pictures on the Internet, especially social media. Be careful. Be discerning."

Reflections for the Day:

_____

_____

_____

_____

_____

_____

_____

Fruit #109: "You can't possibly want full deliverance if you're walking around telling half-truths."

Reflections for the Day:

_____

_____

_____

_____

_____

_____

_____

_____

_____

_____

_____

_____

Fruit #110: "Your state of mind is more important than your state of life. It is your mind that is powerful enough to change your state of life, only if you think right."

Reflections for the Day:

_____

_____

_____

_____

_____

_____

_____

_____

_____

_____

_____

Fruit #111: "The first indication that you're about to elevate is how the attitudes of people around you change. Pay attention."

Reflections for the Day:

_____

_____

_____

_____

_____

_____

_____

_____

_____

_____

_____

Fruit #112: "Some people are legends in their own mind, especially coming from pulpit participants. Be sober in your mind (Romans 12:3). Think humbly about yourself and your vocation. Don't get above yourself. Ever."

Reflections for the Day:

_____

_____

_____

_____

_____

_____

_____

_____

_____

_____

Fruit #113: *"One winter I helped shovel and plow snow from the front doors of my home, our neighbor's home, out of the neighborhood streets, and even around my church. This was about twenty hours of work. My reward was not money or accolade. It was simply the idea that my family, neighbors, and friends could move about with freedom and liberty, not being held hostage in their homes. This is exactly what Jesus the Christ did for us. Because of His life, death, and resurrection we are no longer held hostage to our earthly homes (our bodies, flesh). His reward is our salvation and liberty."*

Reflections for the Day:

_____

_____

_____

_____

Fruit #114: "Because it is for my good doesn't mean that it

doesn't hurt."

Reflections for the Day:

_____

_____

_____

_____

_____

_____

_____

_____

_____

_____

_____

_____

Fruit #115: "Guard your heart because from it flow the

issues of life."

Reflections for the Day:

_____

_____

_____

_____

_____

_____

_____

_____

_____

_____

_____

_____

_____

Fruit #116: "Don't waste your time fighting broke enemies who have nothing to offer. There are no spoils to collect when you defeat them. No, if you're going to fight then be sure it's worth the fight, your time, and your energy."

Reflections for the Day:

_____

_____

_____

_____

_____

_____

_____

_____

_____

_____

Fruit #117: "During your season of preparation this is what you should be doing: 1.) Repair your weak parts (focus on strengthening your weaknesses), 2.) Strengthen your support systems (empower those who support you), 3.) Touch up your image (improve your projections or reinvent yourself), and 4.) Record your progress."

Reflections for the Day:

_____

_____

_____

_____

_____

_____

_____

_____

Fruit #118: "For every person who decides not to support

you, God will give you another person who will support

you one hundred times more than them."

Reflections for the Day:

_____

_____

_____

_____

_____

_____

_____

_____

_____

_____

_____

Fruit #119: "Don't fall behind. Stay on course."

Reflections for the Day:

Fruit #120: "If you outsource anything to someone make certain that they are qualified, competent, and efficient. And always give an estimated time of expected finish."

Reflections for the Day:

_____

_____

_____

_____

_____

_____

_____

_____

_____

_____

Fruit #121: "Whether you think so or not you've got people. These people love you, support you, care or cared for you, want the best for you, respect you, and even got your back. You got people. Thank God you've got people."

Reflections for the Day:

_____

_____

_____

_____

_____

_____

_____

_____

_____

Fruit #122: "My best mistakes are those which have been

erased by the blood of Jesus Christ. That means all of

them."

Reflections for the Day:

_____

_____

_____

_____

_____

_____

_____

_____

_____

_____

_____

_____

Fruit #123: "It's amazing how people who don't know you want to stake claim in your success; and the people who do know you don't want to be associated with your failure."

Reflections for the Day:

_____

_____

_____

_____

_____

_____

_____

_____

_____

_____

_____

Fruit #124: "Always walk in these virtues: humility, honor

of Christ, worship, praise, obedience, love, and faith."

Reflections for the Day:

_____

_____

_____

_____

_____

_____

_____

_____

_____

_____

_____

_____

Fruit #125: "If it took my father walking out of my life at five years old just so that I could become the man that I am today then I wouldn't change a thing. I'd live the entire experience all over again. All of those times that he broke his promises. Each time he cussed me out. The times that we never played ball in the yard, went fishing, and even the times we never had pertinent conversations about life and development. Even the times he never said, "I'm proud of you son." Yes, I would do it all again if that meant I'd get to grow into the man of God I am today. "All things work together for your good (Romans 8:28)."

Reflections for the Day:

_____

_____

_____

_____

_____

Fruit #126: "Sometimes you just want to re-live your childhood and be innocent again. I've learned that salvation gives you that chance."

Reflections for the Day:

_____

_____

_____

_____

_____

_____

_____

_____

_____

_____

_____

Fruit #127: "When you have folks—supposedly friends—

backstab you on the job or in life in general your first

thought ought to be to pray for them."

Reflections for the Day:

_____

_____

_____

_____

_____

_____

_____

_____

_____

_____

_____

_____

Fruit #128: "What were the names of the ten spies who brought back an evil report, telling the children of Israel that they could not possess their promised land? Exactly! No one really knows and no one really cares. Negative people are a dime a dozen. Forget about them and their negative reports. Go in and possess everything that God has said is yours!"

Reflections for the Day:

_____

_____

_____

_____

_____

_____

_____

Fruit #129: "Build the foundation right and everything else

you place on top will stand."

Reflections for the Day:

_____

_____

_____

_____

_____

_____

_____

_____

_____

_____

_____

_____

_____

Fruit #130: "Beware of people who want to control your

life; but want to be free to live their own."

Reflections for the Day:

_____

_____

_____

_____

_____

_____

_____

_____

_____

_____

_____

_____

Fruit #131: "Beware of people who use fear and skepticism

to control you."

Reflections for the Day:

_____

_____

_____

_____

_____

_____

_____

_____

_____

_____

_____

_____

Fruit #132: "Beware of those who seek to control your life through these open doors: gifts, promotions, positions, access, sex, special attention, money, façade concerns, and soul ties or relationships. Be sure that none of these things have unhealthy strings attached."

Reflections for the Day:

_____

_____

_____

_____

_____

_____

_____

_____

_____

_____

Fruit #133: "You're better than a handout. Remember

that."

Reflections for the Day:

_____

_____

_____

_____

_____

_____

_____

_____

_____

_____

_____

_____

Fruit #134: "Girls and boys here's a bit of fatherly advice for you. Before you take a picture of how fly your new hair or new outfit is and go to posting it on social media; please remember to clean up your house first. See, your messy bed, your dirty room, and all of the out-of-order things in your picture speak volumes about who you really are. Whether you know it or not, your character is on display."

Reflections for the Day:

Fruit #135: "Let's do the math of your life. Add up your ability, education, and contacts. Subtract all of your failures, mistakes, and shortcomings. Then divide all of your mistrust, shortcoming and struggles to forgive. Now multiply it with all of your money, assets, health, family, faith, joy, favor, and all of God's goodness in your life. The end result: nothing but God's grace and mercy."

Reflections for the Day:

_____

_____

_____

_____

_____

_____

_____

_____

Fruit #136: "A few years ago, my wife and I owned six investment properties. When the financial market crashed, we lost all of them. Over one million dollars gone just that quick. The preachers kept saying, "Turn to your neighbor and say I'm not participating in the recession." Honestly, I could not say that. I mean, even if I did not want to I was already participating. My deliverance came when I had released all of my properties from my heart. I had to make a choice that the loss of them would no longer stress me. What are you trying to hold on to that is literally killing you? You may just need to let it go."

Reflections for the Day:

_____

_____

_____

_____

Fruit #137: "The enemy will try to stress you out of a good marriage, a good job, relationship, vision, education, purpose, and every good and perfect gift that God has given you. Be prayerful at all times."

Reflections for the Day:

_____

_____

_____

_____

_____

_____

_____

_____

_____

_____

_____

_____

Fruit #138: "Every 45-90 days require an evaluation of yourself, your family, your friendship circles, your ministry, and all else that is connected to you. If we are to make a difference where we are this is a must."

Reflections for the Day:

_____

_____

_____

_____

_____

_____

_____

_____

_____

_____

_____

Fruit #139: "How many believers need love, discipline, direction, and teaching; but instead they get churched, positioned, turned out by their gifts, caught up in the system of religion? Most people are empty when they leave our churches. It's time for real transformation."

Reflections for the Day:

_____

_____

_____

_____

_____

_____

_____

_____

Fruit #140: "Like a one-hundred-dollar bill that has been walked on, dropped in the trash, spit on, and laid in the dirt for ten years; it still retains its value when found by someone who know exactly what it is. Your self-worth is who you are and God gave this to you. Like this one-hundred-dollar bill, your negative experiences will not determine your destiny, the amount of favor on your life, or the joy you receive and bring to others. You are still worth every cent you were born with."

Reflections for the Day:

_____

_____

_____

_____

_____

_____

Fruit #141: "Some of the best advice I've given is, "Get some rest." I often struggle to adhere to my own advice. Perhaps you have trouble with finding rest as well. Although it is hard to do sometimes—please remember—it is necessary. Your body wasn't built to keep going without rest. Rest refuels. "

Reflections for the Day:

_____

_____

_____

_____

_____

_____

_____

_____

Fruit #142: "People are not what they say, they are what

they do."

Reflections for the Day:

_____

_____

_____

_____

_____

_____

_____

_____

_____

_____

_____

_____

Fruit #143: "When was the last time someone offered you a twenty-five million dollar deal for your God-given gift? Until they do, you don't really understand what superstars and celebrities are going through. So pray for people who carry more weight than you do. They have a greater responsibility while being in the spotlight. They are expected to live perfect lives with human limitations that are impossible to say the least. They are literally human corporations. Most of these people are responsible for hundreds of lives. Can you imagine for a moment, no privacy at any time? All day you have to meet demands, deadlines, and consider new concepts to just maintain or risk falling back into obscurity and poverty. Now I'm not making excuses for them. Just shedding some light. Food for thought."

Reflections for the Day:

Fruit #144: "I can't stand—no I hate—church services that start late! It's very disrespectful to my time, my person, my God, and the people who came on time. Guess I just feel like speaking my mind today."

Reflections for the Day:

_____

_____

_____

_____

_____

_____

_____

_____

_____

_____

_____

_____

Fruit #145: "You don't have to compromise the Word of

God in order to promote."

Reflections for the Day:

_____

_____

_____

_____

_____

_____

_____

_____

_____

_____

_____

_____

_____

Fruit #146: "You can't drive to a convenience store and buy self-confidence. The grocery store doesn't have discipline or character on sale. All things must come into manifestation by way of process."

Reflections for the Day:

_____

_____

_____

_____

_____

_____

_____

_____

_____

_____

_____

_____

Fruit #147: "It would blow your mind to know how many

people are praying for you!"

Reflections for the Day:

_____

_____

_____

_____

_____

_____

_____

_____

_____

_____

_____

_____

_____

_____

Fruit #148: "When you are destined for greatness, it demands that you know it. It demands your attention."

Reflections for the Day:

_____

_____

_____

_____

_____

_____

_____

_____

_____

_____

_____

_____

Fruit #149: "You can't bring everybody with you."

Reflections for the Day:

_____

_____

_____

_____

_____

_____

_____

_____

_____

_____

_____

_____

Fruit #150: "When you reach a certain level of greatness and influence you will be responsible for the livelihood of others, their mortgages, car notes, children's private school education, insurance, and so much more. Tell me, can you really carry this type of weight on your shoulders? You must be able to carry your own weight and the weight of others on certain levels of greatness. Next time you ask to be great on a grand scale, consider this. Then ask again if you dare."

Reflections for the Day:

_____

_____

_____

_____

_____

_____

_____

Fruit #151: "If you're on your cell phone at home, then you are not really at home are you? If you are on your cell phone during a date, then are you really on a date? If you are in church talking on the cell phone, then are you really into the service? You more than likely aren't. Improper use of cell phones can get you out of the moment. When you're out of the moment you can often miss God and the things that are transpiring in the spiritual realm. Put the phone down sometimes and pay attention."

Reflections for the Day:

_____

_____

_____

_____

_____

_____

Fruit #152: "Food and lack of exercise is killing most

church folks."

Reflections for the Day:

_____

_____

_____

_____

_____

_____

_____

_____

_____

_____

_____

_____

_____

_____

Fruit #153: "Egypt had its Civil War. Syria had its Civil War. If we don't pray, America will have its modern day Civil War. Republicans taking up arms against Democrats. The rich taking up arms against the poor. The employed taking up arms with the unemployed. Whites and Blacks against one another. Police and ethnic groups are clashing. Yeah, we're headed for a real Civil War if we don't pray fast and make some adjustments spiritually, domestically, and politically. CALLING ALL PRAYER WARRIORS!"

Reflections for the Day:

_____

_____

_____

_____

_____

Fruit #154: "When giving up is not in your heart to do,

then don't give up."

Reflections for the Day:

_____

_____

_____

_____

_____

_____

_____

_____

_____

_____

_____

_____

_____

Fruit #155: "Your doctor's objective is not to cure you, but to treat you. Hence, why he keeps prescribing you medication. He has to sell medicine. The objective of your faith is to get you cured. I'll take faith over medicine anytime."

Reflections for the Day:

_____

_____

_____

_____

_____

_____

_____

_____

_____

_____

Fruit #156: "The pain that you feel, the anger that wouldn't heal, the disappointments, the joy, the triumphs, all of it is the wonderful wisdom of God wrapped up in one mechanism called LIFE. Keep living."

Reflections for the Day:

_____

_____

_____

_____

_____

_____

_____

_____

_____

_____

_____

_____

Fruit #157: "When your capacity is a ten gallon and the people you hang out with have a capacity of one pint there's a problem. They don't have the capacity to think, agree, visualize, or even conceptualize on your level. You're unequally-yoked."

Reflections for the Day:

_____

_____

_____

_____

_____

_____

_____

_____

_____

_____

Fruit #158: "Here's a wisdom I've learned: when someone you love very deeply is really close to someone who hates you deeply—with no valid justification—then don't love deeply, love with suspect."

Reflections for the Day:

_____

_____

_____

_____

_____

_____

_____

_____

_____

_____

Fruit #159: "Listen, learn, and live the abundant life!"

Reflections for the Day:

_____

_____

_____

_____

_____

_____

_____

_____

_____

_____

_____

_____

_____

_____

Fruit #160: "You might not understand what He's doing in your life, but He knows what's best for you."

Reflections for the Day:

_____

_____

_____

_____

_____

_____

_____

_____

_____

_____

_____

_____

_____

Fruit #161: "I can remember being at a very prominent

Pastor's Leadership Conference years ago. The

conference had ended on a Saturday around 3:00 PM. I

made my way back to the hotel and laid down to rest. I can

still remember jumping out of my sleep in a panic.

Somehow, my mind had convinced me that I had slept until

6:00 AM the next morning—which was a Sunday—and that

I only had a few minutes to get to the airport to catch the

next flight out. I was convinced that I would miss our

11:00 AM Sunday service at my church. I threw my things

in the suitcase, brushed my teeth, washed up, and rushed

down to the main lobby of the hotel. I ran out of the hotel

trying to hail a cab to get to the airport, but then I noticed

that it was many people outside for it to be 6:00 AM. So I

asked the gentlemen standing at the front door for the time.

He confirmed that it was indeed 6:00 PM in the evening on

Saturday. I was humiliated. Somehow, my mind convinced

me that it was 6:00 AM the next day. The moral of this

story is: The mind is a powerful thing. It can convince you that something's real when it really isn't at all! So wake up! Don't let your mind trick you into believing a lie."

Reflections for the Day:

_____

_____

_____

_____

_____

_____

_____

_____

_____

_____

_____

_____

Fruit #162: "In my ignorance, I would show up at millionaire's events—thinking I had arrived—but really I was just an asset to them. Every time I showed up, I only made them richer. Your presence must be a mutual benefit."

Reflections for the Day:

_____

_____

_____

_____

_____

_____

_____

_____

_____

_____

12

Prayer

Fruit #163: "Have you ever had to pray after a broken heart? Here's what I said, "Lord, teach me how to find and gather the pieces of my broken heart. Teach me how to pick up the pieces of rejection, denial, grief, patience, but most of all forgiveness. Lord, I need forgiveness for both them and me. Lord, help me learn to trust again. Teach me how to mend and to repair the breach with those I have hurt too. Lord, teach me how to love again. I want to love myself and what I see. Teach me how not to walk in shame, guilt, and condemnation. And Lord, after you've shown me how to pick up the pieces could you put the broken pieces back together again? May my heart beat again. May my heart love again. Thank you Father."

Reflections for the Day:

_____

_____

_____

_____

_____

_____

_____

_____

_____

_____

_____

_____

_____

_____

_____

Fruit #164: "Praying and worrying have something in common. They both desire for a change to be made. Praying is trusting God to make the change. Worrying is wishing the situation will change. Believers pray. Those who have no hope worry."

Reflections for the Day:

_____

_____

_____

_____

_____

_____

_____

_____

_____

Fruit #165: *"Lord God, I decree that all evil, wicked, and corrupt systematic structures will unravel in the light for all to see. May financial, educational, political, religious, and sexual power institutions—that discriminate, manipulate, and control the lives of the disenfranchised—be revealed."*

Reflections for the Day:

13

Relationships

Fruit #166: "Man of God, you can't lie to her at home; and then declare to her the truth in the pulpit. You can't cheat on her in the streets; and then command respect from her behind closed doors. You can't make the church your mistress in public; and then demand her to submit as a wife at home."

Reflections for the Day:

_____

_____

_____

_____

Fruit #167: "Stop going to wells that have no water. The frustration you're experiencing with people is that you keep going to certain people—expecting them to give you a certain thing—but they have no capacity to give it."

Reflections for the Day:

_____

_____

_____

_____

_____

_____

_____

_____

_____

_____

Fruit #168: "Some people are not created to stay in your life forever. They're sent to be repaired or restored, or to repair or restore you. Know the difference."

Reflections for the Day:

_____

_____

_____

_____

_____

_____

_____

_____

_____

_____

_____

Fruit #169: "A double minded man, is unstable in all his ways (James 1:8). Let's be clear sir, you will preach to her; but you will never reach her. She might stay in the house; but the house is not her home. She might serve in the church because she loves God; but she will never support you—as the Man of God—from her heart. Yes, you may have her body; but her heart doesn't belong to you. I call it emotional emptiness and relational abandonment; and it's not of God. Pay attention to her."

Reflections for the Day:

_____

_____

_____

_____

_____

_____

_____

Fruit #170: "Waiting on someone to love you who doesn't have the capacity to do so, is like going to a social event early and awaiting the start of the event only to have gone on the wrong day. The event will never start because you're in the right place at the wrong time."

Reflections for the Day:

_____

_____

_____

_____

_____

_____

_____

_____

_____

_____

Fruit #171: "Some of us take risks when it comes to love; but it's the wrong risk. We'd rather risk the welfare of our dignity and our own self-worth because we'd rather be in love with a lie."

Reflections for the Day:

_____

_____

_____

_____

_____

_____

_____

_____

_____

_____

_____

Fruit #172: "How can you be too weak to break it off with

him, but strong enough to make it comfortable for him?

Know your worth and know your strength."

Reflections for the Day:

_____

_____

_____

_____

_____

_____

_____

_____

_____

_____

_____

_____

Fruit #173: "To all of my sisters and daughters out there:

I'd rather lose a man because I know my self-worth, than to

lose my self-worth because I'm his little secret."

Reflections for the Day:

_____

_____

_____

_____

_____

_____

_____

_____

_____

_____

_____

Fruit #174: "To My Ministers of the Gospel,

I'm sure we all can agree that ministry requires a level of

sensitivity, support, and care. But there's a very thin line

between pastor and parishioner relationships and soul ties

that are beyond such boundary. When you get to a point

where you're fulfilling his or her needs and fantasies—and

vice versa—then you've crossed the line. You've committed

emotional adultery even though you've committed no

sexual act. And if you don't check this at the door, then

this relationship could easily move from platonic to

erotic."

Reflections for the Day:

_____

_____

_____

_____

Fruit #175: "I was twenty-two years old riding down the street one day. I saw that someone had thrown away their old air conditioner. I stopped and put it in my car to take it home. For three years I enjoyed the comfort of someone else's "junk." It is said that, "the most beautiful woman or man in the entire world is your ex on the arms of another." Appreciate them while you have them; and watch what you throw out. Because you no longer want them doesn't mean they're junk."

Reflections for the Day:

_____

_____

_____

_____

_____

_____

_____

Fruit #176: "Effective communication in relationships require that you not only discover how to hear each other's words; but that you also discern each other's feelings. Listen to what they feel inside instead of what they're saying."

Reflections for the Day:

Fruit #177: "Sometimes they want someone to hold them

even when they know it's a lie. Some would risk loving a

lie because they feel it is better than not being in love at all.

Don't be an asset to this toxicity."

Reflections for the Day:

_____

_____

_____

_____

_____

_____

_____

_____

_____

_____

_____

_____

Fruit #178: "Wouldn't it be just wonderful if people came with spec sheets or warning labels. That way all of their worst characteristics could be revealed before you enter into a serious relationship with them. Unfortunately, their flaws are not as obvious if you're not looking with spiritual eyes of discernment."

Reflections for the Day:

_____

_____

_____

_____

_____

_____

_____

_____

_____

Fruit #179: "So your significant other left. Question. Did you make it impossible for them to stay? Oh yeah? How can you treat someone you supposedly love worse than someone you hate? Tell me, why would they stay with you? Remember, when you fail to use a thing for its proper use its called abuse."

Reflections for the Day:

_____

_____

_____

_____

_____

_____

_____

_____

_____

_____

Fruit #180: "When a man doesn't stand by his wife he leaves her uncovered. When a woman doesn't stand by her husband she leaves him open and susceptible."

Reflections for the Day:

_____

_____

_____

_____

_____

_____

_____

_____

_____

_____

_____

_____

_____

Fruit #181: "How many times do we miss God's blessing

because they're not packaged as we expected?"

Reflections for the Day:

_____

_____

_____

_____

_____

_____

_____

_____

_____

_____

_____

_____

Fruit #182: "When your emotional capacity is twenty-five feet deep and the person you're in a relationship with is only willing to go three feet deep, you have a problem. These are the things you need to examine at the beginning of the relationship. You may not be a match for each other. You could save a whole lot of time by coming into this revelation quickly."

Reflections for the Day:

_____

_____

_____

_____

_____

_____

_____

_____

14

Revelation

Fruit #183: "You can be in the will of God and still not know where you're going. You can be uncertain in your direction and still head in the right direction. All it takes is trust. Sometimes the only thing you have is faith. Just imagine the emotional turmoil Abraham had to endure. People were following him and he didn't know where he was going yet. His wife was barren and he was of old age. Yeah, Abraham's a good example of faith in the midst of uncertainty. You don't have an excuse. DON'T GIVE UP! Instructions and directions aren't validation of the promise. It's only the indicator that you're getting closer to it. You'll know it when you see it.

Revelation for the Day:

_____

_____

_____

_____

_____

_____

_____

_____

_____

_____

_____

_____

_____

_____

_____

_____

Fruit #184: "I drove past a fruit tree in my neighborhood one day. I immediately got a revelation. The fruit is not for the tree. You'll never catch a fruit tree eating its own fruit. That's because the fruit produced is for the hungry that passed by it."

Reflection for the Day:

_____

_____

_____

_____

_____

_____

_____

_____

_____

_____

Fruit #185: "The price of freedom can be very costly. But most of the time the freedom is worth it."

Reflections for the Day:

_____

_____

_____

_____

_____

_____

_____

_____

_____

_____

_____

_____

_____

Fruit #186: "You've been called to the Kingdom for such a time as this. You have purpose. Now tap into it and get moving! The Lord has need of thee!"

Reflections for the Day:

_____

_____

_____

_____

_____

_____

_____

_____

_____

_____

_____

_____

Fruit #187: "'In my Father's house are many mansions. If it were not so, I would have told you. For I go to prepare a place for you...' Have you ever stopped to ask, "Why would there be mansions inside of His father's house? Surely a house can fit into a mansion; but a mansion cannot fit inside of a house. Ah yes, the inexhaustible wisdom and revelation of God is at work here. All of humanity's mansions cannot fill even one room in our Father's house. This is why He's able to do exceeding abundantly and above all that we ask or think. God is bigger than you could ever imagine. So take the limits off of Him."

Reflection for the Day:

_____

_____

_____

_____

Fruit #188: "Here's a mystery: After nine months in the womb a baby never breaks the umbilical cord. Never break the line that feeds you."

Reflections for the Day:

_____

_____

_____

_____

_____

_____

_____

_____

_____

_____

_____

_____

_____

Fruit #189: "A dog is said to be able to understand every language in the world. This brings me to a great point. Language barriers are only as strong as your mental capacity."

Reflections for the Day:

_____

_____

_____

_____

_____

_____

_____

_____

_____

_____

_____

Fruit #190: "When you ask God for a tree He gives you a seed. Plant it and watch it grow into a tree. Then watch that tree grow into a forest. As time goes on you'll see that forest manifest into many wood products that can be sold as goods. Here's the point: Ask God for a million dollars and He'll give you a dream. Plant it and watch it grow into a business. If you work it long enough the business will bear fruit of major credit lines, valuables, assets, benefit packages, and the like. Ask God for a ministry and He'll give you a vision. If you plant it and work it long enough, the vision will bear fruit of saved souls, partners, success, and much more. Consider what you've asked God for. You just might have the answer already; but have done nothing with it. Every answer God gives is in the form of a seed."

Reflections for the Day:

_____

_____

_____

_____

_____

_____

_____

_____

_____

_____

_____

_____

_____

_____

_____

_____

_____

_____

_____

Fruit #191: "My goodness, haven't we become doom dumping dogmatic dissing, poisonous venom and bitterness seed dropping, believers. We've reduced the Word of God to a tool of personal vendettas. Wow! Our Lord must be shocked at how Christians can't get along now-a-days."

Reflections for the Day:

_____

_____

_____

_____

_____

_____

_____

_____

_____

_____

Fruit #192: "The cross was His to bear, but the liberty is

ours to share."

Reflections for the Day:

_____

_____

_____

_____

_____

_____

_____

_____

_____

_____

_____

_____

_____

Fruit #193: "I once heard someone say, "I have proof that Jesus wasn't crucified." I said, "Sorry, but I have proof he was. Just look at me. I'm living proof that He died and rose again."

Reflections for the Day:

_____

_____

_____

_____

_____

_____

_____

_____

_____

_____

15

<u>Sin</u>

Fruit #194: "Beware of those who sin with you. For the

right price they'll sin against you."

Reflections for the Day:

_____

_____

_____

_____

_____

_____

_____

_____

_____

Fruit #195: "I needed some clarity concerning what we call Christianity. So I prayed for understanding and here's what the Word revealed to me: If a man is in an adulterous affair or a woman repeatedly steals from people but confesses to be a church-going believer, the only difference between them and the unbeliever is that they go to somebody's church. Question. How can I be God's witness if I'm purposely walking in disobedience? Practicing sin puts you in direct opposition with faith. Either I'm in the dark about what the Word teaches on Christianity or some type of foul myth is warping the minds of this generation. I believe it's the latter."

Reflections for the Day:

_____

_____

_____

_____

Fruit #196: *"I was arriving at the Orlando, Florida airport one day and was pressed for time. It was close to my flight takeoff; so I was very much in a hurry. As I drove through the airport, I begin to see signs directing me to the place I needed to deliver my rental car. Now because of my time restraint I was a bit apprehensive; but I continued. As I kept going, I noticed that I was driving over some metal spikes that were at the entrance of the rental car area. As I kept rolling forward, the metal spikes would go into an offensive mode and release down so that I could continue to come through. However, after each tire would past I noticed that the spikes would pop back up in a defensive mode. This meant if—at any given time—I chose to go in reverse and roll backward then I would have destroyed the tires on the car. The metal spikes would have punctured each tire causing them to immediately go flat. This is as it is with sin. When one gets into the practice of sin it's always easy to get in; but you'll pay a major price when you try to get out of its web. See, practicing sin has the power to blind, bind, and hold captive its prey and victim. The allurement, attractions, entertainment, support systems, the systematic synergies, the thrill of privacy and secrecy; even the instant gratification all work together in conjunction. They work together to hold you hostage to sin. Now let's be perfectly clear, when I'm talking about sin I am not referring to simple deeds that you've committed because of inevitable human error; but rather I am referring to the practice of a behavior. It is the lifestyle, the habitual violation, the continued action that will eventually hold you hostage; and like those metal spikes try to destroy you if you attempt to bail. The parties, the hype, the perpetuation of degrading and senseless music, the lifestyle of sex outside of marriage, the drugs, the lifestyle of alcoholism. All of it starts with a little desire to go in and experience the instant gratification; but it's hard to get out of it. See, it's easy to get into sinful habits and lifestyles; but it can be rough coming out. Sin will always try to make you pay more than you wanted to pay. That's why it's very vital —with the help of the Holy Spirit—that we gain control over sin and our unhealthy habits; rather than allowing it to have control over us. The way you gain control by the Spirit is by learning to choose the right areas to drive into. Just like I had to do at the Orlando airport. Here's a nugget for you: just follow the signs of Christ and His word. That's a sure roadmap that'll get you to the right place every time.*

"Enter ye in at the strait gate: for wide is the gate, and broad is the way, that leadeth to destruction, and many there be which go in thereat:

Because strait is the gate, and narrow is the way, which leadeth unto life, and few there be that find it."

Matthew 7:13-14 (King James Version)"

Reflections for the Day:

_____

_____

_____

_____

_____

_____

_____

_____

_____

_____

_____

_____

_____

_____

_____

_____

Fruit #197: "We are naughty by nature. Our old man is in agreement with it. That's why we should keep our nature on lock down. If not, then you'll see this kitten turn into a lion, Dr. Jekyll turn into Mr. Hyde, or this monkey turn into a gorilla. Be careful."

Reflections for the Day:

_____

_____

_____

_____

_____

_____

_____

_____

_____

_____

Fruit #198: "If the works of the flesh are viewed as a struggle—and we go on practicing that behavior as a lifestyle—then we are fooling ourselves. If our position is that "God understands my situation" then I ask you; is it really a struggle or practice (choice)? What is the difference between struggle and practice? To struggle means to exert strenuous efforts against resistance or opposition: to strive or to progress with effort, difficulty, or a battle contest. A child struggles to walk. An adult who has leg injuries struggle to regain mobility. A practice; however, is a habit, a custom, a method of doing something to perfect a skill or action. Let's be real, nine times out of ten you're not struggling. You've simply made a choice to allow this to be a habit and a pattern. That's why it's been so hard to let go. Your habitual violation has perfected the stronghold in your life."

Reflections for the Day:

_____

_____

_____

_____

_____

_____

_____

_____

_____

_____

_____

_____

_____

_____

_____

_____

Fruit #199: "The power of Sin: We really don't understand the power of sin until we try to break from its relentless, ruthless, never-ending, systematic vicious cycle which dominates your every waking moment. Sin will make you pay more than you want to pay; and stay longer than you want to stay. Sin is not just a sin because it transgressed the laws of God; and violates His very nature of holiness. Rather, in addition to this sin penetrates, contaminates, mutates, and obliterates everything it touches. Yes, even you and me. Avoid sin. You do this by drenching your life in God's Word and getting occupied with pursuing His will."

Reflections for the Day:

_____

_____

_____

Fruit #200: "You'll never appreciate the liberty and peace of righteousness until you walk away from the hindrance of practicing sin."

Reflections for the Day:

_____

_____

_____

_____

_____

_____

_____

_____

_____

_____

_____

Fruit #201: "It's no longer a struggle when you constantly

do it. It is a committed act."

Reflections for the Day:

_____

_____

_____

_____

_____

_____

_____

_____

_____

_____

_____

_____

_____

_____

Fruit #202: "God doesn't have a certain number of mercies He will give you. His mercies for you are limitless. You will never exhaust them. God has a super abundance and supply of mercy. If you need more just ask. Now run tell your haters that!"

Reflections for the Day:

_____

_____

_____

_____

_____

_____

_____

_____

_____

_____

Fruit #203: "Each time you go through something challenging it takes something out of you; but each time you praise it puts something in you. Praise glorifies God, and it fortifies you."

Reflections for the Day:

_____

_____

_____

_____

_____

_____

_____

_____

_____

_____

_____

Fruit #204: "I'm so thankful that my soul is not in the hands of an evil group of church people or a wicked humanity. I'm so glad that my life isn't controlled or governed by those who have no sense of humanity or compassion for anyone but themselves and their own. We are so judgmental at times as a people. This is as if we are without fault."

Reflections for the Day:

_____

_____

_____

_____

_____

_____

_____

Fruit #205: "All of those people who hated you, hurt you, and who purposely did you wrong are now in need of your strength and anointing to sustain them. This is your Joseph Season. Now handle your business by healing those who hurt you. You're stronger than you think you are. You're bigger than you say you are."

Reflections for the Day:

_____

_____

_____

_____

_____

_____

_____

_____

_____

16

Spiritual

Fruit #206: "Be careful what you practice before others. What might be a one-way ticket to heaven for you; can be a one-way ticket to Hell for them. The Apostle Paul speaks about us being careful not to be partakers in another man's sin. Leaders, we must not use our spiritual liberty and freedom to sin against God or our fellow man. We lead people astray when we frivolously sin in front of them. Many believers watch the behavior of their leaders very closely. They often measure their lives by the actions of their leader. So if you're on the frontline, and many who follow you bear corrupt fruit; then you might need to check what you're projecting and modeling before them. Remember, the way you live your life might be the only revelation that someone will ever receive of God."

Reflections for the Day:

_____

_____

_____

_____

_____

_____

_____

_____

_____

_____

_____

_____

_____

Fruit #207: "Christ went to Hell for us so that He wouldn't

have to go back to Heaven without us."

Reflections for the Day:

_____

_____

_____

_____

_____

_____

_____

_____

_____

_____

_____

_____

_____

Fruit #208: "How is it that for centuries we can believe what the Word of God says as it relates to sin; but then relinquish all morals and values now that a new age has ushered into our world? Is it that God's Word has changed to accommodate today's new normal? NO! Or is it that our culture has made us alright with the idea of "if it feels good; then it's good." Saints, either we are going to believe the Word of God or not! 1 John 2:16 says,

"For everything in the world--the lust of the flesh, the lust of the eyes, and the pride of life--comes not from the Father but from the world."

- *1 John 2:16 (New International Version)*

"For all that is in the world, the lust of the flesh, and the lust of the eyes, and the pride of life, is not of the Father, but is of the world."

- *1 John 2:16 (King James Version)*

This scripture indicates to me that everything in the world is based on feelings and emotions; not spiritual things. So I ask you, "If the State legalizes prostitution or theft; has God changed on his position with this matter? I tell you, the perilous times in which the Bible speaks about are here! We are more tolerant in regards to the sins of the world now more than ever. Especially in America. What was once acknowledged as sin; is no longer labeled as such. Let's be clear, although we have been saved by Grace and accepted His freedom; we must remember that where there are liberties there's tendency and proclivity toward abuse. Freedom to a child can feel good at first; but quickly become their worst enemy. Freedom with moral and ethics is called Christianity. Away with this anarchy spirit!"

Reflections for the Day:

_____

_____

Fruit #209: "American capitalism—I call it greed—has deep control over the interpretation and revelation of the scriptures the minister has. Money, trade, and power is about the extent of most of the Church leader's revelation. Thus, we run our ministries with greed and corruption-centered messages. Over the years, this has created a somewhat pseudo-type of Christianity. I call it American Christianity. American Christianity is neck deep entrenched in the American dream. That dream which supports the idea "Capitalism over Christ." So my question is this: At what point does the American Dream (Capitalism over Christ) and "the blessings of the Lord maketh us rich" separate? Just a thought. At some point, we've got to consecrate the Church again; and clean up our messages. We live by the order and economy of the Kingdom of God; not capitalism. When we start preaching Kingdom economic principles; we'll realize that the

American Dream is far less than how God really wants to

bless us."

Reflections for the Day:

_____

_____

_____

_____

_____

_____

_____

_____

_____

_____

_____

_____

_____

_____

Fruit #210: "Has holiness become so outdated that we can't even recognize it? When we see it we quickly call it something else these days."

Reflections for the Day:

_____

_____

_____

_____

_____

_____

_____

_____

_____

_____

_____

_____

_____

Fruit #211: "Every misunderstood experience in your life is God's way and expression of love for you. He knows what's best for you."

Reflections for the Day:

_____

_____

_____

_____

_____

_____

_____

_____

_____

_____

_____

_____

_____

Fruit #213: "Have you ever won a soul for the Kingdom?

Is this something that the Church even does anymore?

What are we doing? If it's not about winning souls for

Christ, then what is it all about? Don't be a selfish

Christian. Share the wealth. God wishes that none would

perish."

Reflections for the Day:

_____

_____

_____

_____

_____

_____

_____

_____

_____

_____

Fruit #214: "Is your house in order? No, I mean your

spiritual house? Jesus is coming soon."

Reflections for the Day:

_____

_____

_____

_____

_____

_____

_____

_____

_____

_____

_____

_____

Fruit #215: "If the Rapture came tonight would you be

ready?"

Reflections for the Day:

_____

_____

_____

_____

_____

_____

_____

_____

_____

_____

_____

_____

_____

Fruit #216: "Did you know that Abraham had eight sons altogether? However, his second son was the promise. Isaac was the promise! The anointing of the second son will preach! There's an anointing on the second sons. Isaac, Jacob, Ephraim, the Christ, and the believers are all considered 'second sons.'"

Reflections for the Day:

_____

_____

_____

_____

_____

_____

_____

_____

_____

Fruit #217: "There's a fire that burns within me that I cannot explain. There's a fire within me that I cannot contain. It's a fire that's raging. It's fueled by my passion for Christ and my yearning of wanting more. The more I yearn, the more I burn for His will in my life."

Reflections for the Day:

_____

_____

_____

_____

_____

_____

_____

_____

_____

17

Spiritual Abuse

Fruit #218: "Spiritual abuse is real. It often comes in the form of control and manipulation; wrapped in religion. Some people use religiosity to control others; especially those closest to them. May I say, these are the same people who have no control over their own lives."

Reflections for the Day:

_____

_____

_____

_____

_____

Fruit #219: "A man who has no control over himself is like a city without walls. He has no limitations, no boundaries, no borders to define how far he will go. A man with no control is like a knife. He will take the truth and cut you open for the purpose of killing you. The man with self-control takes the truth in his hands; and cut you open for the purpose of healing you.

Reflection for the Day:

_____

_____

_____

_____

_____

_____

_____

_____

_____

_____

_____

_____

_____

_____

_____

_____

_____

18
Spiritual Wisdom

Fruit #220: "When I was a child we lived in a basement apartment, and every time it rained our apartment would flood. Finally, my mom was approved for an apartment in the projects on the third floor. Now many wealthy people in our city perceived the projects to be a step down, but to my family, the projects were a step up and out of the mess where we resided. Here's the lesson: Celebrate! Because where you are might seem bad, but remember that's only your perception because of where you stand. Looking at it from someone else's view; it could be worse. Just always keep this is mind: where you're going is better than where you've been. Your trial may be someone else's triumph.

It's all about perspective."

Reflections for the Day:

Fruit #221: "Until you get sick and tired of being sick and tired; you'll remain sick and tired."

Reflections for the Day:

_____

_____

_____

_____

_____

_____

_____

_____

_____

_____

_____

_____

_____

Fruit #222: "At some point you've got to stop praying,

"Lord, what am I doing wrong," and start telling yourself,

"Self, get up and move along." Indecisiveness is not the

will of God for you. Stop waiting on God. God's waiting

on you to make an intelligent move."

Reflections for the Day:

_____

_____

_____

_____

_____

_____

_____

_____

_____

_____

Fruit #223: "Be careful not to be your own worst enemy."

Reflections for the Day:

_____

_____

_____

_____

_____

_____

_____

_____

_____

_____

_____

_____

_____

_____

_____

Fruit #224: "If I take an object and throw it at you with all of my might; more than likely you'll defend yourself from it. As it is with the truth; which is the Word of God. If I took it and threw it at you with all of my might; then you'd defend yourself from it too. But if I hand you the truth without threat of harm, more than likely you'd receive it with open arms."

Reflections for the Day:

_____

_____

_____

_____

_____

_____

_____

_____

Fruit #225: "Destiny is a tag team sport. If you don't meet the people that are sent—by God—to push you into your destiny, then frustration will set in. Bitterness, anger, and resentment could consume you. This is why divine networking is imperative. Hook up with your divine team of pushers. Together you all could push one another into greatness."

Reflections for the Day:

_____

_____

_____

_____

_____

_____

_____

_____

Fruit #226: "Stop trying to drag your drama into your destiny. It just don't fit! And—hey—if it don't fit; don't force it!"

Reflections for the Day:

_____

_____

_____

_____

_____

_____

_____

_____

_____

_____

_____

Fruit #227: "You're being disturbed into your destiny."

Reflections for the Day:

_____

_____

_____

_____

_____

_____

_____

_____

_____

_____

_____

_____

_____

_____

_____

_____

Fruit #228: "A part of a famous man's story was his wife catching him cheating with another woman. His infamous words to her were, "Who are you gonna believe? Me or your lying eyes?" Here's the moral of the story. When people show you the caliber of person that they are; then believe them! People will tell you anything; but it's their behavior that speaks the truth. If you commit a crime what's on trial is not what you say; but rather what you've done. Actions speak louder!"

Reflections for the Day:

_____

_____

_____

_____

_____

_____

_____

Fruit #229: "You are a gift from God to the world, so wrap yourself in the most striking wrapping paper possible. Some can't receive you because they can't see you. Dress the way you want to be addressed."

Reflections for the Day:

_____

_____

_____

_____

_____

_____

_____

_____

_____

Fruit #230: "Educate your mind each day."

Reflections for the Day:

_____

_____

_____

_____

_____

_____

_____

_____

_____

_____

_____

_____

_____

_____

Fruit #231: "Appreciate, affirm, and show attention to

others."

Reflections for the Day:

_____

_____

_____

_____

_____

_____

_____

_____

_____

_____

_____

_____

Fruit #232: "Here's a myth for you: the spiritually gifted are super-humans. NEWS FLASH! Spiritually gifted people are not super-human. They struggle too."

Reflections for the Day:

_____

_____

_____

_____

_____

_____

_____

_____

_____

_____

_____

Fruit #233: "Remember, pride attracts empty people."

Reflections for the Day:

_____

_____

_____

_____

_____

_____

_____

_____

_____

_____

_____

_____

_____

_____

_____

_____

Fruit #234: "I found out something about a lie. It makes

angry those it tells the truth on."

Reflections for the Day:

_____

_____

_____

_____

_____

_____

_____

_____

_____

_____

_____

_____

_____

_____

Fruit #235: "Your strength is in your ability to admit that you have a weakness."

Reflections for the Day:

_____

_____

_____

_____

_____

_____

_____

_____

_____

_____

_____

_____

_____

_____

Fruit #236: "Your power is in avoiding temptation that leads to entanglement. You're stronger than you think you are."

Reflections for the Day:

_____

_____

_____

_____

_____

_____

_____

_____

_____

_____

_____

_____

_____

Fruit #237: "If you fail to open your hands and give; then your hands are closed and can't receive. If you fail to believe God with your dollar; then He will give someone else your economy. Wealth transfers to those who are open and ready to receive (Proverbs 13:22)."

Reflections for the Day:

_____

_____

_____

_____

_____

_____

_____

_____

_____

_____

Fruit #238: "Just as your body needs food and water because it's hungry and thirsty; so does our soul and spirit need the presence of God. His presence is life unto our spiritual bodies."

Reflections for the Day:

_____

_____

_____

_____

_____

_____

_____

_____

_____

_____

_____

Fruit #239: "There are some mistakes that you learn from.

There are others that alter your life indefinitely. It's your

job to discern which one does what and run like Joseph if

need be."

Reflections for the Day:

_____

_____

_____

_____

_____

_____

_____

_____

_____

_____

_____

_____

Fruit #240: "Sometimes you'll become acquainted with your strength by the weaknesses you've endured and overcome."

Reflections for the Day:

_____

_____

_____

_____

_____

_____

_____

_____

_____

_____

_____

_____

Fruit #241: "When your desire is aroused you won't seek advice. You will crave satisfaction. Period. So before your desire is aroused install the security alarm system of wisdom. This is when lust and enticement comes lurking; your alarm system will keep them from breaking and entering your life. Now that's real victory. Prepare for the test; before it even comes."

Reflections for the Day:

_____

_____

_____

_____

_____

_____

_____

_____

_____

Fruit #242: "Often times you can't tell what God is doing in your life; you'll just have to walk it out and let others see. They wouldn't believe you if you said it anyway. Actions speak louder."

Reflections for the Day:

_____

_____

_____

_____

_____

_____

_____

_____

_____

_____

_____

_____

Fruit #243: "Can God trust you with an answer to your prayers? I once prayed for God to take me to my next level. About a month later I received a phone call that my father needed to live with me because of the cancer that was taking over his body. My siblings and I had to do everything for him. We had to carry him to the car, bathe him, feed him, and so much more. This was a trying time. Here's the lesson: when you ask God for your next level; He gives it to you in the form of tests and trials. This is the only way to grow up to the next level. Are you ready?"

Reflections for the Day:

_____

_____

_____

_____

_____

Fruit #244: "When David killed Goliath, King Saul wanted to kill him. Who would've thought that when you killed the giant in your life that it would cause your friends (even your covering) to want to kill you? Success brings out the truth in the people around you."

Reflections for the Day:

_____

_____

_____

_____

_____

_____

_____

_____

_____

_____

Fruit #245: "I was twenty-two years old and saved when I was invited to a Bachelor's Party. I said, "I'll only come if there are no strippers." I arrived and a few minutes later, she jumps out of the bathroom. I got up to leave and she said, "If he leaves then I'm going to stop." This upset the whole party. Well of course, I left. Many years later—one of the guys who was present at the party—gave his life over to God. He said he would only join my ministry because he trusted me as a Pastor. Later he died and went on to glory. Here's the lesson: a decision that might not mean anything to you right now can be a ticket to Hell for someone else. Your destiny is greater than momentary pleasure. Many need you to stand up and make the right choice. Your good choices may introduce them to God's salvation."

Reflections for the Day:

_____

_____

Fruit #246: "Wow! I've tried to live right for more than thirty-six (36) years before I was consecrated a Bishop. I've come up through the ranks; and have done it all in the church. I've cleaned the toilet and preached in pulpits. I've built out rooms, played music, ushered, served on the twenty-four (24) hour security team. I've been the Youth Pastor, the Chaplain, the Vice Chairman, and so much more. Through the years I've had to learn obedience, parliamentary procedures, even had to learn how to shut my mouth and be quiet at times where I so desperately wanted to speak up and speak out. These are all things that I'd do all over again; if I had to. I must admit, I've missed the mark at times. I haven't always dotted every I; nor crossed every T. But the point is; I've tried.

For the most part, I can say that I've been obedient and faithful to the call of serving God. I've done my best to remain faithful and committed to my church, as a Bishop, to my family and friends. I've been tested. Oh yes, talk about tested. I've been examined and placed in front of a group of Elders who judged my preaching three (3) times just to see if I handled the scriptural text with integrity; only to have to wait for one (1) whole year before I could even preach my trial sermon. Years after I had been called to preach; I was tested to get my Ministerial License. I was examined by a group of Elders for ordination, and after many years of pastoring I was examined again by Bishops and Elders; a group of individuals who tested my motives and intentions of being in the ministry. After this, I went back to seminary for two (2) years. At this time, I was placed on trial for two (2) years by being sent to Rome, Italy. I was tested to see if I was worthy of the call of a Bishop, and examined once more at a proclamation service by Bishops who were fathers in the city. I was placed on hold for six (6) months before I was able to walk in the office of a Bishop. During my waiting period, an announcement was placed in the newspaper that made it known I was seeking the office of a Bishop. The community had six (6) months to give their valid reasons as to why I should not become a Bishop.

And after all of this; then I was consecrated a Bishop in the Lord's Church by three of the nation's renown Bishops. They questioned my pastors, friends, and family about my lifestyle. And if anyone knows my wife; they know she will not lie to cover up my wrongdoing or behavior. She will tell the truth; even if that means it's about me. But the point of all of this is not to brag or boast. It's to confirm that—yes—I've been tried and tested on so many levels. And let's not get on the tests and trials of my personal life. God has seen me through many tests.

After all of the examination, I still felt inadequate and unworthy. I still feel as though I'm unqualified at times. I tremble at the notion that I have done this process without God's true calling. What if I wasn't called to this level of ministry? I still shake at the notion that just maybe my *ambition has caused me to step out into an office where I will fail and bring shame to the Father. I have utterly feared the idea that just maybe I was too quick. Perhaps this wasn't the right timing. Will I have to stand before God and answer Him as to why I failed at this work? I'm convinced that many people don't understand the weight and magnitude of pressure this office and ministry period place on a person. I am not sure if **we** understand the weight of **this** office **and these offices** we ascend to; and the eternal judgment that is linked to doing this **in His name**. I am not trying to condemn anybody's ambition, his or her plans or hopes...*

We must know that an office in Christ's Kingdom is not an occupation; but a calling (Hebrews 5:4). I see people selling all sorts of clergy certificates for Prophets, Pastors, and other positions. They even have them on sale for fifty dollars if you want to become a Bishop. Let's be clear, you can't pay for a position or a title. It's a calling. You have to be called to this lifestyle, to this suffering, to this burden.

Ministry is a heavy weight that you must be called to bear.

At times, I still question whether I am able to bear it.

Ministry will place you in the eye of judgment every single

day, every hour, every minute, and sometimes every second

of your life. Not to mention that with the office come

testing, trial, sufferings and attacks: mentally, emotionally,

intellectually, and spiritually. Your energy, your time, your

gifting, your skills; all will be put to the test. Can I mention

the countless hours of prayer, the hours of fasting, the non-

stop discipline to study to show yourself approved (2

Timothy 2:15). Ministry is continued growth and

advancement. Not to mention if you produce fruit; God

will always purge you. The more you produce, the more

He will purge you. That is just principle. This is only so

you can produce on a more effective and abundant level.

Each day you go on the quest of seeking normalcy; while

friends, foes, family, and such look at your every move.

Yes, the ministry can be perplexing.

Yet, there is something else that has given me peace about

my call; that is the countless lives that have been

transformed. The souls won. This gives me hope and

encouragement. My calling and my constant obedience to

Christ is not in vein. I have done it all for the Kingdom;

just so that I might win some. Moreover, I can surely

testify and say that thousands have received Christ because

of my humble service to God. When people say, "Bishop

my life has been changed because of you," peace comes

over me. Although the word of God says that, the guard

must answer for the souls he preached to and the life we

have led in front of them; I still have a sense of peace

knowing that someone's life has been transformed because

of the Christ in me. Ministry. Perplexing; yet satisfying."

Reflections for the Day:

_____

_____

_____

_____

_____

_____

_____

_____

_____

_____

_____

_____

_____

_____

_____

_____

Fruit #247: "You don't have time to watch someone else's

life while trying to live your best life."

Reflections for the Day:

_____

_____

_____

_____

_____

_____

_____

_____

_____

_____

_____

_____

_____

_____

Fruit #248: "Envy is a disease of the spirit. It eats away at your anointing after a while."

Reflections for the Day:

_____

_____

_____

_____

_____

_____

_____

_____

_____

_____

_____

_____

_____

Fruit #249: "Jealousy is controlling in nature. Don't let

the jealousy of others control you."

Reflections for the Day:

_____

_____

_____

_____

_____

_____

_____

_____

_____

_____

_____

_____

Fruit #250: "Hatred is like drinking venom and waiting for

the rat to die."

Reflections for the Day:

_____

_____

_____

_____

_____

_____

_____

_____

_____

_____

_____

_____

_____

_____

Fruit #251: "God has not given us the spirit of fear (2 Timothy 1:7). So you can give attention to the threat all you want by swatting at it like a fly. But keep in mind, you can wreck the car trying to do that. Don't let fear get you on the side of the road; or worse killed."

Reflections for the Day:

_____

_____

_____

_____

_____

_____

_____

_____

_____

Fruit #252: "When my sons were just toddlers I took them across the street to play in the yard. After we were done, we began to walk back home hand-in-hand. One son was on the right and the other on the left. Just as we approached the curb I didn't trust that they would continue to hold my hand as we crossed the street so I grabbed the both of them by their arms. Listen, when you don't feel the Father's hand it's because He is holding you tight around your arms until you are safely out of harm's way. He will keep you even when you don't want to be kept."

Reflections for the Day:

_____

_____

_____

_____

_____

_____

Fruit #253: "Allow me to get real. Until God has kept you when you didn't even want to be kept, you don't know what real victory is."

Reflections for the Day:

_____

_____

_____

_____

_____

_____

_____

_____

_____

_____

_____

_____

Fruit #254: "What if I told my two sons to, "Stay in this house and don't leave," but a fire broke out in the house while I was not there. Should my sons leave or stay? I hope that they would know my character and my ways enough to know that I would not want them to die in the fire. Therefore, it is in the spiritual. You may know God's words; but it's imperative that you know His character and His ways too."

Reflections for the Day:

_____

_____

_____

_____

_____

_____

_____

Fruit #255: "If you are a child of God then you should bear His name and his characteristics. You can't love Him and hate others. God rejects those who lie on Him and say they're apart of His family; but bear none of His fruit."

Reflections for the Day:

_____

_____

_____

_____

_____

_____

_____

_____

_____

_____

_____

_____

Fruit #256: "Sometimes you learn how weak you are by

how much His grace and mercy extends for you."

Reflections for the Day:

_____

_____

_____

_____

_____

_____

_____

_____

_____

_____

_____

_____

Fruit #257: "Here's a wisdom for you: we are perfectly imperfect. We have flaws for the purpose of being perfected through faith."

Reflection for the Day:

_____

_____

_____

_____

_____

_____

_____

_____

_____

_____

_____

_____

Fruit #258: "Your position in Christ is how God sees you.

Your condition in Christ is what Satan uses against you;

but it is God who uses both your position and condition to

bring you to full fruition."

Reflections for the Day:

_____

_____

_____

_____

_____

_____

_____

_____

_____

_____

_____

Fruit #259: "I am very particular about what I allow to touch my face and what I allow to touch my body. As it is in the natural, so it is in the spiritual. The Lord will allow certain believers to touch His body; while only a select few can stand in His face. It's all about what material you're made of."

Reflections for the Day:

_____

_____

_____

_____

_____

_____

_____

_____

_____

_____

Fruit #260: "There are many people who feel that I have a great ministry. They rant and rave over my preaching, my teaching, my anointing, my worship center; but none of this is important. I've come to realize that if my wife and sons don't feel this way about me; then I'm actually a failure. My first ministry begins at home with those who see my humanity. They see who I really am. Wonder what your closest loved ones think about you behind closed doors?"

Reflections for the Day:

_____

_____

_____

_____

_____

_____

_____

Fruit #261: "I once saw a movie where the leading man was comparing his scars with his female counterpart. He showed her a scar and she said, "Well if you think that's something look at this." Then she showed him a scar. He then said to her, "Well I've got something worse than that." Then he proceeded to show her another scar. This banter continued for a few moments and it got me to thinking. That is exactly how church folks are. They love being the victim, comparing their scars to that of others in the church. This is an attention-seeker spirit. At some point, we—as a body of believers—have to heal. Stop being the victim and choose to become a victor!"

Reflections for the Day:

_____

_____

_____

_____

Fruit #262: "I AM A WINNER! I hate to lose. That's why I'm glad about the promise where it says, "All things work together for my good (Romans 8:28)." That means, even if it seems like I'm losing I'm actually winning!"

Reflections for the Day:

Fruit #263: "Due to our prosperity Gospel for the past thirty years, we are such babes in Christ. When are we going to get out of 1 Corinthians 12 and step over into 1 Corinthians 13? It's time for a more excellent way!"

Reflections for the Day:

_____

_____

_____

_____

_____

_____

_____

_____

_____

_____

Fruit #264: "You can't change other people unless you start with the man in the mirror."

Reflections for the Day:

_____

_____

_____

_____

_____

_____

_____

_____

_____

_____

_____

_____

_____

_____

Fruit #265: "I used to preach for me, but now I preach for them. It used to be all about appeasing my flesh, but now it's all about transforming souls."

Reflections for the Day:

_____

_____

_____

_____

_____

_____

_____

_____

_____

_____

_____

19

Vanity

Fruit #266: "My son Justin posted on his social media status one day, "I don't see the problem with vanity." My response: My son, here is the problem with vanity. Biblical interpretation says that vanity leads to double emptiness. The key word here is emptiness. You can live your entire life with vain experiences; and when it all comes to an end you'll realize it led to emptiness. Imagine this: You are the only one in your city who can afford to buy a shiny new aluminum garbage can. You are in high regards because of it. Everyone has your name on his or her lips. Everyone desires to have what you have; but of course, not everyone can afford the shiny new garbage can. Imagine living your entire life having the respect, admiration and envy of the entire city; but now you are at the end of your life. Let me ask you a question, "Did your trash can ever love you? Could your trash can ever bring you peace? Was your trash can ever anointed to heal you when you got sick? The real answer is, "No. A trash can—no matter how shiny—doesn't possess those capabilities. The only real effect your trash can had on you was enlarging your ego. The result? Emptiness. Empty in your spirit. Empty in your soul. Empty in your relationships with God and people. All you are left with is an empty shiny aluminum garbage can; and honestly it helped no one. Not even you. All it did was boost your ego. See my son, this is the problem with vanity! It'll leave you shallow and empty inside. Lifeless without real meaning. Think about this. Your shiny new garbage can may be your car, your house, education, your lifestyle. Your shiny new trash can could very well be your new position on the job, your career, your title, the shape of the physical appearance or even your preaching style. Don't be fooled son. All things pertaining to life is empty without God. Nothing means

nothing without God."

Reflections for the Day:

_____

_____

_____

_____

_____

_____

_____

_____

_____

_____

_____

_____

20

Wisdom

Fruit #267: "It's very difficult to remove the silver spoon out of your mouth when you keep putting your foot in it. If you say you're humble—more than likely—you're not. Be certain that what you say about yourself is true because everybody can tell a fake. They just won't tell you."

Reflections for the Day:

_____

_____

_____

_____

_____

_____

Fruit #268: "Your head isn't placed on backwards for a reason. So stop that madness of always looking back over your history. Focus on your destiny. Life is too short!"

Reflections for the Day:

_____

_____

_____

_____

_____

_____

_____

_____

_____

_____

_____

Fruit #269: "Here's a nugget for those who want better for someone who just doesn't want it for themselves. Your deliverance is in realizing that you can only change yourself."

Reflections for the Day:

_____

_____

_____

_____

_____

_____

_____

_____

_____

_____

_____

Fruit #270: "A community of elephants were under attack by a lion in the wild. The lion closed in on their herd trying to attack a baby elephant. One of the female elephants saw this and took immediate action. She used her power and defeated the lion. Nevertheless, another large female elephant lived in a zoo. She was up in arms and going wild in the closed area she resided. To my surprise, she was losing her mind over a small little mouse. Many times, we—humans—are just like that caged elephant in the zoo. We lose our minds over something so small and harmless; and forget our strength to defeat lions, tigers, and even bears. Oh my!"

Reflections for the Day:

_____

_____

_____

_____

Fruit #271: "Stop hating on others because they're engaged in the pursuit of their destiny. Divorce the drama and focus!"

Reflections for the Day:

Fruit #272: "Be careful how you handle people who look up to you. What might mean nothing to you just might mean the world to them."

Reflections for the Day:

_____

_____

_____

_____

_____

_____

_____

_____

_____

_____

_____

_____

Fruit #273: "True deliverance is getting control over what

has been controlling you."

Reflections for the Day:

_____

_____

_____

_____

_____

_____

_____

_____

_____

_____

_____

_____

_____

Fruit #274: "The greatest evidence of power is

transformation."

Reflections for the Day:

21

Words of Wisdom to Men

Fruit #275: "It doesn't take any character to have sex with multiple women. All you need is an apparatus. See, when you are confused about love; then you will love a community of women. You will love the legs on this one, the eyes on that one. You will love the breasts on this one and the butt on that one. However, it takes character to love one woman. It takes character to love all that is within one woman. You do not love her parts, because you are wise enough to know that her parts will change. You love the totality of who she is: mind, body, spirit, and soul."

Reflections for the Day:

_____

_____

_____

_____

_____

_____

_____

_____

_____

_____

_____

_____

_____

_____

_____

_____

_____

Fruit #276: "I've found that it is extremely easy for men to be thugs, yet it's extremely hard for them to be vulnerable. Vulnerability takes maturity. If you have not mastered some level of it, then you have not reached manhood at all. You are still a boy posing as such. Be free."

Reflections for the Day:

_____

_____

_____

_____

_____

_____

_____

_____

_____

Fruit #277: "You know you have the best that God has to give when your wife is your full-time lover, your best friend, your ride or die, the mother of your children, your pastor, your co-worker, your number one cheerleader, your advisor; and she does this all while making you laugh."

Reflections for the Day:

_____

_____

_____

_____

_____

_____

_____

_____

_____

_____

_____

Fruit #278: "The hardest thing about being a father is not caring for your family; but rather, how to stop caring so much about yourself. Fatherhood requires unselfishness and selflessness."

Reflections for the Day:

_____

_____

_____

_____

_____

_____

_____

_____

_____

_____

Fruit #279: "As a boy, if the King in you can slay giants;

then surely as a man the King in you can control the

immaturity of the little boy. As a boy, King David defeated

Goliath. But King David struggled with defeating the woes

of the little boy inside. He never could defeat the spoiled

little boy's cravings who always wanted another man's toy.

Killing a man for his wife was only an example of King

David's inner-boy struggles. What little boy issues are you

struggling with that's working in opposition to your

kingship?"

Reflections for the Day:

_____

_____

_____

_____

_____

_____

Fruit #280: "With tears in my eyes and a thump in my chest—father to father—if you have small children then cherish them at that age. Most of all please be patient with them. Allow them to be children. Spend as much time as you possibly can playing, running, and teaching them all that you know. Take time to get to know them. Get to understand their pain, their joys, and all that is in between. All of the precious moments are a must because—before you know it—the moment will vanish."

Reflections for the Day:

_____

_____

_____

_____

_____

_____

Fruit #281: "Men are like trucks. There are Tonka Trucks where the man has the mind of a child. He thinks that the noise he is making with his mouth and all of the games he plays is what matters most. Then there is the Pick-up Truck. He is the hustler. He is always picking up junk on the street and laying anyone on the back-end that will fill his tank. He is more than likely not financially stable. His career is hustling. Then there is the Dump Truck. These guys carry heavy burdens for you. They move mountains for you. Nevertheless, they will only go so far. They often make dependable money; but aren't adventurous. Then there are the men who are Tractor Trailers. There is no distance too far for him. If you are cold, he will warm you up. If you are about to spoil he will cool you off. He will remove his back-end for you and ship it around the world by airplanes, trains, and ships. He doesn't bring home checks. He has bank transfers."

Reflections for the Day:

22

Words of Wisdom to Women

Fruit #282: "When driving out of the captivity of your past; the objects in your rearview mirror are closer than they appear. Do not fail to signal when changing lanes and moving forward; because rushing up behind your bumper is a six-foot-two-inch fine man. He drives a BMW with a six-figure income. He has the swagger. He has the charm. However, what he doesn't have is the Almighty God. Watch what is in your rearview mirror and blind spot when switching lanes and moving forward. An accident is bound to happen if you do not be careful. Moreover, before you know it, he will have your phone number and the keys to your heart. A man who doesn't have the heart of Christ doesn't deserve your heart, and he certainly doesn't deserve your slowing down on the road to greatness."

Reflections for the Day:

Fruit #283: "Here it is. Another holiday or major event is approaching and your stomach is in knots. You already can hear the argument you're about to have. You know, that one about whether he's going to spend the night with you or go home to his wife and kids. As beautiful as you are, you are his dirty little secret. Woman, you deserve better. God has someone just for you; but you've got to want better for yourself."

Reflections for the Day:

_____

_____

_____

_____

_____

_____

About the Author

John R. Thompson Sr. is an American Pastor, Gospel Artist, Author, and Inventor *(holds a US- Patent for the EZ Brush toothbrush)*. He is the Bishop, Founder and Senior Pastor of Calvary Temple Christian Center located in Bridgeport, Connecticut and the Presiding Prelate of the International Royal Priesthood Fellowship of Churches. John R. Thompson has been married to the love of his life and his Co-Pastor, Jenice R. Thompson, for thirty (30) years. Together they have two sons, John R. Thompson II, Justin R. Thompson, and a granddaughter Jeniel Renee Thompson.

BishopJohnRThompson | @BishopThompson7 | BishopThompson7

Dudley Publishing House

www.dphouse.net

Made in the USA
Middletown, DE
17 May 2017